Listening Without Borders

T0276948

WRITING WITHOUT BORDERS

Writing Without Borders exists to provide space for writing and thought which challenge the norms of academic discourse. Books in the series will touch on Multilingual Matters' key themes – multilingualism, social justice and the benefits of diversity and dialogue – but need not focus entirely on them. Books should be short (20,000–40,000 words is ideal) and represent a departure in some way from what and how you would usually write a journal paper or book manuscript. They may contain experimental writing, new ways of thinking or creating knowledge, topics that are not generally addressed in academic writing or something we haven't thought of yet... The series is a place to explore, think, challenge and create. If you are not sure if your idea is 'right' for this series, please ask us.

Writers from the Global South will be particularly welcomed and sought out, as well as writers from marginalised communities and groups within the Global North. Writers from all academic disciplines are welcome, as are experts working in non-academic settings.

Full details of all the books in this series and of all our other publications can be found on http://www.multilingual-matters.com, or by writing to Multilingual Matters, St Nicholas House, 31-34 High Street, Bristol, BS1 2AW, UK.

WRITING WITHOUT BORDERS: 3

Listening Without Borders

Creating Spaces for Encountering Difference

**Edited by
Magdalena Kubanyiova
and Parinita Shetty**

**with Louise Dearden
and Ana Korzun**

MULTILINGUAL MATTERS
Bristol • Jackson

DOI https://doi.org/10.21832/KUBANY1053
Library of Congress Cataloging in Publication Data
A catalog record for this book is available from the Library of Congress.
Names: Kubanyiova, Magdalena, editor. | Shetty, Parinita, editor.
Title: Listening Without Borders: Creating Spaces for Encountering Difference/Edited by
    Magdalena Kubanyiova and Parinita Shetty.
Description: Bristol; Jackson: Multilingual Matters, [2024] | Series:
    Writing Without Borders | Includes bibliographical references and index. |
    Summary: "This book asks what it means and what it takes for people to
    encounter one another ethically, beyond the boundaries of what is
    shared, in settings where ideological systems and imaginations clash. It
    engages over 40 contributors across geographies, disciplines, art forms
    and practices in a conversation which the reader is invited to join"—
    Provided by publisher.
Identifiers: LCCN 2024012738 (print) | LCCN 2024012739 (ebook) |
    ISBN 9781788921046 (paperback) | ISBN 9781788921053 (hardback) |
    ISBN 9781788921060 (pdf) | ISBN 9781788921077 (epub)
Subjects: LCSH: Multiculturalism—Moral and ethical aspects. | Social ethics. Classification:
    LCC HM1271 .L495 2024 (print) | LCC HM1271 (ebook) |
    DDC 305.8—dc23/eng/20240409 LC record available at https://lccn.loc.gov/2024012738
LC ebook record available at https://lccn.loc.gov/2024012739

British Library Cataloguing in Publication Data
A catalogue entry for this book is available from the British Library.

ISBN-13: 978-1-78892-105-3 (hbk)
ISBN-13: 978-1-78892-104-6 (pbk)
ISBN-13: 978-1-78892-106-0 (pdf)
ISBN-13: 978-1-78892-107-7 (epub)

Open Access

Multilingual Matters
UK: St Nicholas House, 31-34 High Street, Bristol, BS1 2AW, UK.
USA: Ingram, Jackson, TN, USA.

Website: https://www.multilingual-matters.com
X: Multi_Ling_Mat
Facebook: https://www.facebook.com/multilingualmatters
Blog: https://www.channelviewpublications.wordpress.com

The policy of Multilingual Matters/Channel View Publications is to use papers that are
natural, renewable and recyclable products, made from wood grown in sustainable forests.
In the manufacturing process of our books, and to further support our policy, preference is
given to printers that have FSC and PEFC Chain of Custody certification. The FSC and/or
PEFC logos will appear on those books where full certification has been granted to the printer
concerned.

Typeset by Deanta Global Publishing Services, Chennai, India.

Contents

Contributors

Elisabetta Adami, PhD, is associate professor in multimodal communication at the University of Leeds, UK. Her research in social semiotic multimodal analysis has a current focus on culture, interculturality and translation. She has published on sign-making practices in place, on urban visual landscapes and superdiversity; in digital environments, on intercultural digital literacies, aesthetics, interactivity and social media practices; and in face-to-face interaction, in intercultural contexts and deaf–hearing interactions. Her latest volume is *Multimodal Communication in Intercultural Interaction* (2023, Routledge), co-edited with Ulrike Schroeder and Jennifer Dailey-O'Cain. She is a founding editor of the journal *Multimodality & Society* (SAGE), former editor and on the editorial board of *Visual Communication* (SAGE) and *Multimodal Communication* and leads Multimodality@Leeds.

Mohasin Ahmed is a public health practitioner, community organiser and DJ. Their previous work looks at community-led initiatives to addressing health inequalities and meaningful community engagement in research. They are interested in transformative justice, specifically for queer and racialised communities and they have an abundance of experience working and volunteering within local grassroots organisations. They are also the founder of Exhale.group, a non-profit aiming to create spaces to dream, explore and connect for QTIPOC+ living in Scotland.

Nadra Assaf is the founder/artistic director of the Al-Sarab Dance Foundation. She is an advocate for the arts in the Middle East and is also a full-time academic (Lebanese American University) and a well-known researcher of dance in the Middle East. Among her publications: '(Re)Positioning, (Re)Ordering, (Re)Connecting: A Choreographic Process of Mind and Body Convergence' (2022); 'Audience/Performer Re-Action: An Investigation Into Audience/Performer Reciprocity via a Touring Site-Specific Performance in Lebanon' (2020). In 2016, she started an atypical collaboration with American dancer, professor and choreographer

Heather Harrington; their most recent performance: Mirror, Mirror... how they fall, in the 2023 edition of WADEintoActivism.

Ingrid Rodrick Beiler is an associate professor of English at Oslo Metropolitan University (Norway). She researches multilingualism, literacy, internationalisation and the status of English, with particular emphasis on transnational students' language socialisation trajectories. Through her work, she has contributed to renewed consideration of student translation practices and highlighted the dual role of English as a facilitator and gatekeeper of educational opportunities. Her current projects include collaborative research on multilingual approaches and digital language teaching in adult basic education. In the ETHER network, she has also drawn on previous experience from civil society and educational work in the United States, Palestine and Iraq.

Gert Biesta is professor of educational theory and pedagogy in the Moray House School of Education and Sport, University of Edinburgh, Scotland, and professor of public education in the Centre for Public Education and Pedagogy at Maynooth University, Ireland. He writes about the theory of education and the philosophy of educational research, with a strong interest in democracy, citizenship, teaching, curriculum and education policy. In 2023, he was appointed to the Education Council of the Netherlands, the advisory board of the Dutch government and parliament.

Adrian Blackledge is professor of sociolinguistics at the University of Stirling. He conducts ethnographic research in the field of language in society, with a particular focus on multilingualism and translanguaging. He is currently developing creative approaches to the representation of research outcomes. He is author or editor of 14 books about his research. The latest of these is *Essays in Linguistic Ethnography: Ethics, Aesthetics, Encounters* (2023, Multilingual Matters), with Angela Creese. He was poet laureate for the city of Birmingham from 2014 to 2016.

Cornelia F. Bock is a PhD researcher in African linguistics at the Universität Hamburg, Germany. Her dissertation (submitted) focuses on the relationship between language, identity and religion in a German-African church service. Recent publications include a special issue on the sociolinguistics of exclusion in mobile communities (Bock, Busch & Truan, 2023), an article on the motif of crossing borders in intercultural sermons (Bock, 2023) and an ethnographically informed analysis of (written) language practices and ideologies at a medieval fair (Bock & Busch, 2021).

Gail Boldt is a distinguished professor of education in the Department of Curriculum and Instruction at Penn State. She teaches graduate seminars in theory and philosophy as they relate to contemporary issues in education. At the undergraduate level, she works in the Elementary and Early Childhood programme, teaching literacy methods classes for pre-K–4th grade pre-service teachers. She is an affiliated faculty member in women's, gender and sexuality studies. She is the senior editor of the Bank Street Occasional Paper Series. She is also a psychoanalytically oriented psychotherapist, trained in providing play therapy to children.

Tracey Costley is a senior lecturer in English language teaching (TEFL/TESOL) in the Department of Language and Linguistics at the University of Essex. In her research, she largely adopts ethnographic approaches in exploring and understanding language learning and teaching with a particular focus on how teachers and students come together to create and construct meaning. She is interested in how language policies shape and are shaped by classroom and community practices, and how individuals' linguistic repertoires are (or are not) drawn upon in teaching and learning. She works with concepts such as multilingualism, translanguaging and superdiversity in her work.

Angela Creese is professor of linguistic ethnography in the Faculty of Social Sciences at the University of Stirling. She is an experienced researcher and is committed to reflecting on the processes, possibilities and challenges of producing knowledge in team research. Her research interests are in sociolinguistics, multilingualism and interaction in everyday life. A recent publication with Blackledge called *Essays in Linguistic Ethnography* (Multilingual Matters) has created a new avenue of research into relational ethics and arts-based research.

Louise Dearden is an EAP teaching fellow at the University of Birmingham. Prior to this, her career spanned three decades in the field of language education and drama, working across a diverse range of educational contexts in Europe and the UK. Her varied experience has allowed her to explore how people learn and communicate at the intersection of language and the arts, and how creative pedagogies have the potential to open spaces for meaningful engagement in the classroom. Louise is a PhD researcher whose research was conducted at an adult education institute in the UK where she was teaching migrant learners. This interest led her to ETHER where she joined the research team as a postgraduate project assistant.

Ana Deumert is professor of linguistics at the University of Cape Town. Her research programme is located within the broad field of sociolinguistics and has a strong transdisciplinary focus. Her current work explores the use of language and art, especially sound and music, in global political movements as well as the contributions that decolonial thought can make to sociolinguistic theory. Recent publications include *Colonial and Decolonial Linguistics – Knowledges and Epistemes* (2020, with Anne Storch and Nick Shepherd) and *From Southern Theory to Decolonizing Sociolinguistics* (2023, with Sinfree Makoni). She is a recipient of the Neville Alexander Award for the Promotion of Multilingualism (2014) and the Humboldt Research Award (2016).

Joke Dewilde is professor of multilingualism in education and head of research at the Department for Teacher Education and School Research at the University of Oslo, Norway. Her research interests include multilingualism at the margins, multilingual literacies, and multicultural school and community events. She is concerned with developing creative methodologies, drawing on perspectives from critical sociolinguistics and linguistic ethnography. Currently, Dewilde leads a research project commissioned by the social entrepreneur Magisk Kunnskap who has developed a multilingual digital learning platform for immigrant students.

Anna Frances Douglas is a curator, researcher and writer with a particular interest in the practices and theories of visual media, particularly photography in its many forms (that she terms 'photographies') and filmic media. Over the past 10 years, she has curated five major photographic-based projects engaging little-known archives and collections of 'documentary' and 'record' photography, unsettling, shifting and expanding received historical and interpretive narratives of photographic meaning, highlighting the medium's polyvocality. She considers and argues in her PhD-by-practice that curating is a research practice, through which counter-narratives and new knowledges about media images can be uniquely accessed.

Jonathan Dove, winner of the 2008 Ivor Novello Award for classical music, has written more than 30 operas of different shapes and sizes. These are regularly performed all around the world, including the highly successful airport comedy Flight. He has written operas for a family audience (The Adventures of Pinocchio, The Enchanted Pig, Swanhunter, Itch), and works bringing together amateur and professional performers (Tobias and the Angel, The Monster in the Maze). He has received two RPS Awards, two British Composer Awards and has been Featured Composer in festivals in the UK, Europe and the United States. He was made a Commander of the British Empire (CBE) in the Queen's 2019 Birthday Honours for services to music.

Dagmar Dyck is a first-generation New Zealander of Tongan, German, Dutch and Polish ancestry. She is an interdisciplinary artist, primary school art educator and social justice advocate. Her navigation in and around different worldviews is at the heart of her identity, arts and teaching practice. Dagmar's artistic career spans 30 years of regularly exhibiting nationally and internationally, with her works held in both significant public and private collections in New Zealand. Her current academic research seeks to reposition the critical role that the arts can play in addressing persistent disparities in educational outcomes for Pacific learners.

Charlotta Palmstierna Einarsson is associate professor of English literature at Mid-Sweden University, Sundsvall. Her research interests include modernist literature, drama and dance studies, aesthetics, affect theory, philosophy and phenomenology. She is the author of *A Theatre of Affect: The Corporeal Turn in Samuel Beckett's Drama* (2017) and *Beckett's Drama: Mis-Movements and the Aesthetics of Gesture* (2024).

Kate Fellows wants to change the whole world for the better using museum collections. She has worked with object-based learning in museums for a range of organisations from the National Trust to Harewood House and IWM North, and is currently the head of learning and access for Leeds Museums and Galleries. She was the 2010–2011 learning fellow on the Clore Cultural Leadership programme, is the chair of the Group for Education in Museums (GEM) Yorkshire and Humberside and the Yorkshire Accessible Museums Network, founding member of GLAM-Cares, a trustee for Artlink West Yorkshire and moderates for Artsmark.

Helen Finch is professor of German literature at the University of Leeds. She works on queer memory, memory of the Holocaust, life writing and contemporary German literature. Her most recent monograph, *German-Jewish Life Writing in the Aftermath of the Holocaust: Beyond Testimony*, appeared in 2023. Her current research is driven by these questions: What are the power relationships and ethics involved in translating literature about the Holocaust between languages? How can the practices and art of queer memory be used to create knowledge and resilience for creative worldmaking? How can German studies support students to build critical, creative and courageous communities?

Charles Forsdick is Drapers professor of French at the University of Cambridge and a professorial fellow of Murray Edwards College. From 2012 to 2021, he was AHRC theme leadership fellow for translating cultures. He researches and teaches on a range of topics, including travel writing, postcolonial literature, colonial history and translation. He is currently British Academy lead fellow for languages.

Amber Galloway graduated from San Antonio College with an AAS degree in interpreting for the deaf, subsequently earning her BA in psychology, and her master's degree in ASL/English interpreting. After interpreting in many different capacities (staff/freelance/video relay) and in a variety of settings, Amber felt the need to give back to her profession by teaching and advocating for access in entertainment. Amber is busy interpreting concerts and music festivals in a myriad of genres under her company: Amber G. Productions.

Thandanani Gumede ('Thanda') is an award-winning vocalist (Parliamentary Jazz Award Jazz Ensemble of the Year 2023), Jazz Album of the Year 2023 nominee as part of UBUNYE and a multidisciplinary artist of dual Zulu/Xhosa heritage from Durban, South Africa, currently based in England. Additionally, Thanda is an Opera North pilot BAME Resonance Alumnus; mjf Hothouse Alumnus; mjf Level Up Alumnus; co-founder of the dance troupe Zulu Tradition; former arts and creative engagement officer for Manchester Jazz Festival (2023–2024). He is a vocal tutor, choir leader and practitioner of embodied autoethnography with UK refugee status.

Heather Harrington danced with the Martha Graham Ensemble, the Pearl Lang Dance Theatre and the Bella Lewitzky Dance Company. She created her own contemporary dance company in New York City, performing nationally and internationally. She has been on the faculty at Kean University, Seton Hall University and Drew University. Her artistic and scholarly collaboration with Lebanese dancer and scholar Nadra Assaf has led to performances, articles and conferences across the globe. Her scholarship examining gender and dance, dance as protest, consumer dance and the choreographic process has been published by *Choreographic Practices*, *Dancer Citizen*, *Nordic Journal of Dance*, *Journal of Dance Education*, *Beauty Demands* and *Dance Education in Practice*.

Irene Heidt currently holds the position of substitute professor of English and English language education at BTU Cottbus-Senftenberg, Germany. Previously, she worked as a postdoctoral researcher at the University of Potsdam and as a secondary school teacher of linguistically and culturally diverse students in Berlin, Germany. Her research interest is focused on the development of symbolic competence, decolonial and multilingual perspectives on English language education, critical language teacher education with a particular focus on ethical and political dimensions as well as virtual exchange and critical global citizenship education in EFL.

Sophie Herxheimer is an artist and poet. She has held many residencies in the UK and internationally. Her work has been shown at Tate Modern, the British Library and on a giant mural along the seafront at Margate. She made a 300-metre tablecloth for the Thames Festival, a life-size concrete poem in the shape of Mrs Beeton, and devised the colour palettes for CBeebies shows *In the Night Garden* and *Moon and Me*. Her collection

Velkom to Inklandt (Short Books, 2017) was a *Sunday Times* Book of the Year. Her book *60 Lovers to Make and Do* (Henningham Family Press, 2019) was a TLS Book of the Year. She has an ongoing project where she listens and draws stories live with members of the public. Her latest collection is *INDEX* (zimZalla, 2021), 78 poems made from found text, published as a tarot deck.

Awad Ibrahim is full professor, vice-provost, equity, diversity and inclusive excellence and holder of the Air Canada professorship on anti-racism in the Faculty of Education, University of Ottawa (Canada). He is a curriculum theorist with special interest in applied linguistics, cultural studies, hip hop, youth and Black popular culture, social foundations, social justice, diasporic and continental African identities. He has researched and published widely in these areas. Among his most recent books are *Disruptive Learning Narrative Framework: Analyzing Race, Power and Privilege in Post-Secondary International Service Learning* (2023) and *Nuances of Blackness in the Canadian Academy: Teaching, Learning, and Researching while Black* (2022).

Khadijah Ibrahiim is a published writer, literary activist, interdisciplinary artist and curator born to Jamaican parents. She graduated from the University of Leeds with a master's in theatre studies. The BBC hailed her as one of Yorkshire's most prolific poets. Her work features in poetry anthologies, university journals, on BBC radio and in numerous exhibitions. In 2014, Peepal Tree Press published her book *Another Crossing*. She founded Leeds Young Authors and co-coordinates the Inscribe Readers writers for Peepal Tree Press. She is the recipient of the Leeds Black Awards, the Leeds Black Achievers 'Wings Award' and the Legacy Awards for 'International Impact' and features in *Jamaicans In Britain: A Legacy of Leadership*. She was a Forward Prize judge for best single poem and performance (2023).

Rosine Kelz teaches political theory at the University of Bremen. Her research focuses on theories of temporality and notions of difference. She works on topics at the intersections between social and political thought and the environmental humanities. Rosine was an Andrew W. Mellon postdoctoral fellow in bio-humanities at the University of Illinois at Urbana-Champaign and a research associate at the Institute for Advanced Sustainability Studies in Potsdam. She earned her DPhil at the University of Oxford.

Ana Korzun is a part-time postgraduate researcher at the University of Leeds, exploring the migration and language learning experiences of Baltic women migrants. Originally from Lithuania, Ana spent time in Norway before permanently moving to England to live and teach English as an additional language. Her grandad's tales about trips to Africa inspired Ana's concern for the world, and the experiences she gained living in a culturally, socially and politically diverse environment made her interested in other people's stories. For her PhD project, Ana utilises the extended Framework of Investment (Darvin & Norton, 2015) to explore how migrants learn the language of their host country.

Maggie Kubanyiova is professor of language education at the University of Leeds where she directs the Centre for Language Education Research. Her research cuts across sociolinguistics, education and arts to investigate educational encounters in multilingual settings. She was a principal investigator on an AHRC project, Ethics and Aesthetics of Encountering the Other (ETHER; 2020–2022) and continues to work with educators, students, creatives and third-sector organisations to pursue the practical consequences of this research for individuals and communities. *Under the Big Tree: Šuňiben kamibnaha* (2023; Next Generation Publications) is the outcome of her latest collaboration with Sophie Herxheimer (a UK-based poet and artist) and Anna Koptová (a Slovak-based Romani translator and activist).

Lara-Stephanie Krause-Alzaidi is assistant professor at the Institute of African Studies at Leipzig University. Her PhD from the University of Cape Town, *Relanguaging Language from a South African Township School* (2021, Multilingual Matters), reconceptualises named languages with the help of primary school teachers. She now takes her scepticism of named languages further, questioning the concept of language itself by investigating, from a new materialist perspective, relationships between differently racialised bodies and elements of semiotic landscapes in Germany. She is interested in the materiality of words in relation to different bodies, and in how understanding this relationship can help in encountering the other ethically.

Sarah-Jane Mason is a creative practitioner, facilitator and educator who specialises in using mixed media approaches to personal and participatory arts projects. She believes that creativity is the key that unlocks learning and that play and experimentation are important parts of the creative process. An integral part of her arts practice is working as the director of Lacuna Festivals; an artist-led, annual, international, contemporary art festival. This role enables Sarah-Jane to hold a space for artists and to facilitate an environment where artists and audience members can interact, question, share and otherwise meaningfully engage with each other.

Erin Moriarty is associate professor in deaf studies at Gallaudet University. She is also an honorary research fellow at Heriot-Watt University in Edinburgh and affiliated faculty with the Schuchman Deaf Documentary

Center at Gallaudet. Moriarty's work is situated at the intersection of ethnography and applied linguistics. She studies multilingual, multimodal languaging practices, language ideologies and deaf encounters using visual methods. She has conducted ethnographic research in Southeast Asia since 2009; her current research project focuses on deaf tourist mobilities in Indonesia and the mobile semiotic repertoire.

Thea Pitman is professor of Latin American studies at the University of Leeds, UK. Her research centres on Latinx and Latin American digital cultural production, focusing in particular on questions of identity. She has published *Latin American Cyberculture and Cyberliterature* (LUP, 2007), *Latin American Identity in Online Cultural Production* (Routledge, 2013) and *Decolonising the Museum: The Curation of Indigenous Contemporary Art in Brazil* (Tamesis, 2021), as well as many articles on related topics. Her most recent work has focused on Indigenous appropriations of new media, including generative artificial intelligence tools, as well as ecocritical readings of video games.

Nigel Rapport received his MA from Cambridge University and a PhD from Manchester University. He is emeritus professor of anthropological and philosophical studies at the University of St Andrews where he was founding director of the St Andrews Centre for Cosmopolitan Studies. He has also held the Canada research chair in globalisation, citizenship and justice. His most recent monographs are *Cosmopolitan Love and Individuality: Ethical Engagement beyond Culture* (Rowman & Littlefield, 2019) and *'I am Here', Abraham said: Emmanuel Levinas and Anthropological Science* (Berghahn, 2024), and as editor, *The Routledge International Handbook on Existential Human Science* (2024).

Colin Reilly is a lecturer in linguistics in the Division of Literature and Languages at the University of Stirling and an associate fellow in the Department of Language and Linguistics at the University of Essex. His research focuses on multilingualism, language policy and linguistic ethnography. He is interested in understanding the ways in which language policies can influence access to services, institutions and opportunities in multilingual settings, particularly within education and labour market contexts.

Gehan Selim is the Hoffman Wood chair in architecture at the University of Leeds. She is the deputy director at Leeds Social Sciences Institute and was fellow of the Senator George Mitchell Institute for Global Peace, Security and Justice (2017/2018). She is leading the Architecture and Urbanism Research Group at the University of Leeds with her research covering interdisciplinary methods bridging between architecture, urban politics and digital heritage. She is leading several funded research projects with an extensive portfolio of empirical research in the Global South. She is the author of *Unfinished Places* (Routledge, 2017) and *Architecture, Space and Memory of Resurrection in Northern Ireland* (Routledge, 2019).

Rae Si'ilata is director of Va'atele Education Consulting which delivers NZ Ministry of Education PLD and research contracts to ECE services, primary and secondary schools. Current projects focus on supporting leaders, teachers and learning assistants to utilise heritage languages and cultures within learning spaces, and to promote multilingualism and multiliteracies. During her career, Rae has been a teacher and principal in Aotearoa and Samoa. From 2005 to 2020, Rae worked as a lecturer/senior lecturer at the University of Auckland, supporting teachers with post-graduate study. Since 2020, she has also worked with doctoral students at an Indigenous Māori university: Te Whare Wānanga o Awanuiārangi.

Parinita Shetty is a part-time postdoctoral researcher, a part-time public library assistant and a sometimes children's book writer. She completed her MEd in children's literature and literacies at the University of Glasgow in 2017 and her PhD in education at the University of Leeds in 2022. She launched a PhD research/fan podcast called 'Marginally Fannish' to explore intersectionality and public pedagogy in fan podcasts. Her other research interests include children's literature, young people's agency, critical literacies and online fan communities of popular media. She is passionate about including diverse voices in public, cultural and academic spaces, and finding creative ways to make knowledge accessible to diverse audiences.

Joseph Michael Valente is an associate professor of education at Pennsylvania State University. He is the author of *d/Deaf and d/Dumb: A Portrait of a Deaf Kid as a Young Superhero* (Peter Lang, 2011). He was the co-principal investigator of the video ethnographic study 'Kindergartens for the Deaf in Three Countries: Japan, France, and the United States', funded by the Spencer Foundation. Currently, Dr Valente is the principal investigator of the linguistic video ethnographic study 'Children's Everyday Practices in Inclusive Transglossic Spaces: A Study of Collectivist Approaches to Deaf-Nondeaf Inclusive Bilingual Education in France', funded by the Spencer Foundation.

Quentin Williams is director of the Centre for Multilingualism and Diversities Research (CMDR) and an associate professor of sociolinguistics in the Linguistics Department at the University of the Western Cape (UWC). He was the Ghent visiting professor (Leerstoel Houer) at the Centre for Afrikaans and the study of South Africa at Ghent University (Belgium) in 2022. He is co-editor of the journal *Multilingual Margins:*

A Journal of Multilingualism from the Periphery. His most recent books are *Global Hiphopography* with Jaspal Singh (Palgrave, 2023) and *Struggles for Multilingualism and Linguistic Citizenship* with Tommaso Milani and Ana Deumert (Multilingual Matters, 2022).

Maya Youssef is hailed as 'queen of the qanun' (a 78-stringed plucked zither). She is a globally renowned qanun player and composer from Syria. Born in Damascus, Maya arrived in the UK in 2012, endorsed by Arts Council England as an exceptional talent. Maya's albums received critical acclaim from the media and won the German Record Critics' Award and Songlines Music Award. Alongside the composition and performance aspects of her career, Maya has helped hundreds of Arabic music enthusiasts from all over the world learn the qanun, the modal system of the Arab world and the art of improvisation.

Acknowledgment

This work was supported by the Arts and Humanities Research Council (2020–2022) as an international research network grant 'Ethics and Aesthetics of Encountering the Other: New Frameworks for Engaging with Difference' (AH/T005637/1). Further information is available at https://ether.leeds.ac.uk/

Our thanks go to all, too numerous to name, who have contributed to the larger conversation reflected in this book through their direct and indirect participation in ETHER. This includes all authors featured in this book, all ETHER seminar participants not included in these pages, and all those who gave up their time to share thoughts on earlier versions of this manuscript. We are also grateful to Louise Williams Lewis for assisting the entire team in creating this space for conversation.

We are indebted to Dominic Gray (Opera North) and Kate Fellows and John Donnegan (Leeds Museums and Galleries) whose engaged partnership has been invaluable in bringing particular collaborations and conversations to life.

We extend our gratitude to Anna Roderick from Multilingual Matters whose faith in the book project from the outset was a game changer for us, to the entire production team, especially Stanzi Collier-Qureshy, Flo McClelland and Gomathy Ilammathe, whose meticulousness and patience have been exemplary and, last but not least, to our anonymous reviewers. We do not know your names, but please know that your practice of generous and deeply attentive critique have given us a profound sense of what being neighbours to one another could look like in the academy and beyond. Thank you.

1 Introduction to Listening Without Borders

Magdalena Kubanyiova and Parinita Shetty

This book has grown out of an Arts and Humanities Research Council network titled ETHER (Ethics and Aesthetics of Encountering the Other). We have used language sciences as a starting point for entering into a conversation with disciplines, practices and individuals that inhabit spaces outside of this research domain's typical remit. Over the course of three international seminars online, ETHER has brought together linguists and community activists, architects and artists, philosophers and poets, teachers and curators, musicians, dancers and sign language interpreters. We asked one another what it means and what it takes for people to encounter one another ethically in settings where ideologies and imaginations collide. We listened to one another's perspectives as we considered how these 'big' questions play out in 'small' everyday encounters in classrooms, rehearsal rooms, arts projects, public squares, charity events and city markets. Crucially, ETHER has attempted to forge such encounters in the space of its own (digital) interdisciplinary exchange. *Listening Without Borders*, then, encompasses questions of vital societal concern, a vision for interdisciplinary scholarship and a pedagogy for social action. Our aim is to make its affordances accessible to a wider audience. We do this not by providing answers but by creating a polyphonic flow and inviting the reader to participate by listening – without borders – to its voices.

Urgency, Discomfort and the Need to Refrain from Judgment

What is the point of a book that promises to 'listen' and, worse, offers no conclusions? The conversation on which *Listening Without Borders* is based has grown from the generosity of those who participated in ETHER. This international network was set up to explore an overarching question that meant a lot to all and to each differently: 'How do people of conflicting worldviews, memories and future visions encounter each other?'.

Societal polarisation, racial injustice, colonial injury, the rise of fascism, genocidal trauma, the environmental consequences of the Anthropocene, anti-immigration sentiment, the disintegration of the welfare state, the persistent exclusion of minoritised groups from full participation in society, the erasure of certain bodies from public spaces. These, and others, were the wounds that we, through our experience or our witnessing, carried into our conversations and that animated our reasons for holding them. None of us thought we were going to address the question, let alone right the wrongs. If anything, the current geopolitical era of new forms of violent colonisation lends a renewed urgency to the question. It leaves even less hope of healing or answers. Our ambition, instead, was modest. We came together in the virtual space of three ETHER seminars between 2020 and 2022 to share our attempts (and often failures) to encounter others ethically in the multitude of small and unremarkable rituals of researching, teaching, art making and meeting strangers.

'Stranger', in fact, is an apt frame from which to approach the question and which, to a large extent, informed our approach to the seminars. The space was structured as an invitation to meet – within the parameters of mutual respect but outside the comforts of familiarity – the strangeness and unpredictability of the other's discipline, viewpoint and, often, face.

> I come to the present... by a different route from yours; and therefore, our conversation has to recognise that... different histories have made this conversation possible. I can't pretend to be you. I don't know your experience. I can't live life from inside your head. So, our living together must depend on a... conversation. (Hall, 2007: 151)

And, while many of us brought to this conversation our anthropological and/or artistic sensibilities that routinely ask us to make the familiar strange, inhabiting the tenet from positions of vulnerability when egos are at stake cannot be anything other than an act of foolishness. Unless such discomfort also happens to be an opening (cf. Shetty, 2022) through which the other – the stranger, the neighbour, the fellow human being, the world – can announce themselves and come into our presence.

Listening does not guarantee an ethical encounter. Nothing does. We, humans, are quick learners when it comes to armouring ourselves in effective strategies of performative listening (Bassel, 2017; Connor, 2023), shielding ourselves from the voices of those we cannot (under)stand (Brizić, 2024; Krause-Alzaidi, 2024) or purporting to listen to the other when all we really hear is the noise of our own certainties, foregone conclusions, prejudice and bias (Inoue, 2003; Kubanyiova, 2024; Rosa, 2019; Snell & Cushing, 2022; Williams, 2024). In this book, we use 'listening' as an encompassing metaphor for receptivity, witnessing and affective attunement to the voice, face, body, story, music, touch or language of the other. We invite the reader not to evaluate or make conclusions, but simply to commit to co-presence and pay attention.

> As a reader of these two embedded writers [Seamus Heaney and Toni Morrison], both profoundly interested in their own communities, I can only be a thrilled observer, always partially included – by that great shared

category, the human – but also simultaneously on the outside looking in, enriched by that which is new or alien to me, especially when it has not been diluted or falsely presented to flatter my ignorance – that dreaded 'explanatory fabric'. Instead, they both keep me rigorous company on the page, not begging for my comprehension but always open to the possibility of it, for no writer would break a silence if they did not want someone – some always unknowable someone – to overhear. I am describing a model reader–writer relationship. But… the same values… also prove useful to us in our roles as citizens, allies, friends. (Smith, 2022: xxxv)

The absence of fixed conclusive borders is what this book's premise and promise stand on. An invitation to the reader to exercise similar restraint (cf. Kubanyiova, 2024) may be deeply counter-cultural in some geographical, social or disciplinary spaces. But it is far from new in others, even though its demand on the listener remains radical: to shed the idea that it is only through our *understanding* that the other can be heard. This book unsettles its primacy, from any vantage point, be it cultural, historical, linguistic, socioeconomic. It deliberately runs against the idea of needing to have *the* or even *an* answer *before* one can begin to listen. It disrupts the logic and expectation of an authoritative narrative line *after* one has heard. As soon as a pattern starts emerging, a new line, a new perspective, a new experience, a new configuration, a new tune shakes you (and us) out of it. Just as listening to the music of Bach (Robertson, 2016: 243–246) or Miles Davis (1969) does.

> It's like listening to a train a lot of times; you know, sometimes it's the same and other times it changes. Yes, you can hear different things all the time against it. But watch those people who want to be comfortable, man—they'll turn you in. Who wants to be comfortable?… But your reflexes and ears have to be with it, to take you through. No matter what tempo it is, you have to just feel it right…. But when you get egos involved… you can't do it. (Davis, 1969)

Listening Without Borders is that kind of invitation.

Its call is likely to sound hollow to the ears of the academy, the space from which we, the editors, at least partly speak. The space where status and privilege tend to be the project, rather than relationships (Lillie & Larsen, 2024). This book exists deliberately to undermine this status while, at the same time, raising the question of what is ethical and possible in settings where authoritative solutions, certainties and outcomes dominate talk of 'good science'. This book works overtly with the question of what it might take to 'feel it right' or to practice 'right-way science' (McKemey *et al.*, 2022). Nothing to do with imposing the right conclusion. Everything to do with being the right kind of listener: present, honest, turned to the other and there for the long term. No one is exempt. Everyone has to do the work.

Who the Book Is For and How to Read It

We want this book to reach diverse audiences. Its broader topic is relevant to those committed to creating inclusive environments in classrooms, workplaces and neighbourhoods. It can serve as a resource for an additional layer of reflection to accompany educational, civic and arts organisations in their efforts to diversify their workforce, engage diverse audiences, decolonise their artistic repertoires and cultural collections, and rethink their outreach work. There are no easy answers to any such questions and, as noted, it is not this book's remit to offer any. But its content can sensitise those charged with such responsibilities to issues, stories or voices that can often remain unheard and unaddressed in the rush to tick desired boxes to win arguments or funding. The resource will also be useful as reading material for students and academics across a range of social science and arts and humanities disciplines to expose them to interdisciplinary conversations while providing an opportunity to participate in them, to introduce them to alternative modes of inquiry, engagement with others and writing, and to inspire them as they shape relevant questions for their future research or practice. The conversations in this book can also be used as a springboard to designing new and context-relevant teaching, professional development or community resources for anyone working in such settings wishing to respond concretely and creatively and as they judge appropriate to the central question.

We are fully aware that different audiences, some of which we have named here, might appreciate varied entry points into the material. To this end, we provide at least three distinctive routes to navigating this book's content, including a more detailed overview of the book's structure, a 'pre-index' that matches key questions with page numbers in ways that signal more explicitly relevant contexts of practice, and a list of supplementary material that can be accessed flexibly before, in addition to, or alongside reading relevant parts of this book.

The Content Summary

Chapter 1: Introducing *Listening Without Borders*

This chapter explains the context for the book, our rationale for its format and our method.

Chapter 2: Communicating Within, Between and Beyond Social Categories

Social categories are contextual and contested with no universal understanding that can be applied to all contexts in the same way. In this chapter, deaf, Indigenous and race scholars, museum curators, semioticians, multilingualism researchers, anthropologists, DJs, arts educators, musicians and others discuss how traditional markers of cultural identities can be mobilised to start conversations that challenge cultural assumptions and create openings for meaningful encounters with difference. Facilitating collaborative art, research and interpretation activities can similarly help forge ethical relationships in multilingual and intercultural spaces. But the conversations also engage with uncomfortable dilemmas around social categories: the dangers of undermining historical injustices versus threats of homogenising. The chapter makes visible some of the practices that are deployed to engage with opposing threads of the argument or to communicate across identity categories.

Chapter 3: Encountering through Storytelling

Whose stories are told, who gets to tell them and, just as crucially, who listens? These conversations explore the ethical, aesthetic and political implications of representing diverse experiences. Many people's stories have been historically excluded from different cultural, social and educational spaces. In this chapter, museum curators, educators, researchers, poets, artists, dancers, musicians and sign language interpreters discuss how they or those they work with are reclaiming mainstream narratives. Their counternarratives and practices challenge the erasure of those on the margins and rewrite the default scripts that exclude them – older women in dance spaces, interpreters translating music performances for deaf audiences, underprivileged knowledges in museums, classrooms, books, poetry and popular fictional media. Creative ways of representing research can similarly disrupt academic norms. These opportunities are growing and are exploited by many across these sectors. But the difficult questions linger: Who has the right to tell and what does the responsibility to listen entail? What kind of spaces enable encounters with different stories and help communities tell new histories, futures and possibilities?

Chapter 4: Negotiating Discomfort Together

Encountering others can be deeply disconcerting if one is accustomed to the comforts of familiarity in unchanging environments. Resistances, disagreements and tensions of all kinds can and will show up. How are these discomforts navigated in social interactions? Participants discuss their experiences of failures and frustrations as well as their deliberate pedagogies of discomfort. The conversations show how mistakes, vulnerabilities and uncertainties can open up new and deeper ways of seeing and engaging with others. They acknowledge that such an outcome is never guaranteed but requires active effort, collective listening and persistent negotiation rooted in care for the other.

Chapter 5: Designing Spaces for Encountering Others

In this chapter, the discussion centres on the materiality of spaces. Much is claimed about the so-called 'safe space'. This chapter reflects on how a space becomes 'safe' and who and what can and will make it 'safe'. The conversations highlight how people and institutions structure, reclaim and transform spaces as well as the relationships within them. They challenge the idea of spaces as neutral zones with no agency. They show instead how spaces 'speak' and highlight the responsibility to attend to such signs. The participants examine what inclusion or exclusion looks like in city squares, art studios, museum buildings, shop windows, dance floors, schools and places of worship. They propose creative ways of expanding spatial norms about which bodies belong in which spaces and who has 'the right to breathe in them' (Khadijah Ibrahim, this volume). The conversations engage with challenging dialectics between taking up space, carving out separate but safe alternatives and co-existing in shared spaces. The chapter also illustrates the affordances of online spaces, such as the one that has enabled the conversations curated as part of this book.

A Pre-Index of Sorts

As noted earlier, we believe that the material in this book can be of interest to many, but it does not need to be read in the same way by everyone. For those preferring to focus on conversations that relate to their specific domains of practice, the following pre-index can be a helpful navigation route.

Who is 'other'?

What is an encounter with difference?

What is the role of education?

What is the role of arts?

What is the role of language?

What is the role of story?

Pages 39-41, 44-46, 54-56, 61-64, 66-71, 80-81, 91-92

What is the role of the body?

Pages 18-19, 22-23, 48, 59-61, 74-75, 109-112, 115-117, 120-121

Can music be an encounter?

Pages 29-31, 35-37, 43-44, 61-62, 68, 76-77, 78-79, 83-85, 91-92, 96-97, 108, 117-118

Can arts fail to encounter?

Pages 43-44, 66-68, 89-90, 91-93

How can museums encounter ethically?

Pages 32, 37-38, 64-65, 107-108, 111-112, 119-120

How can public space enable encounter?

Pages 18-19, 37-38, 69-71, 83-85, 98-102, 105-107, 109, 111-118, 120-121

Can research be an encounter?

Pages 24-26, 33-35, 56-57, 71-72, 73-75, 90, 91

What if I don't agree? What if I don't get it? What if I get it wrong?

Pages 24-29, 39-41, 41-43, 47-48, 68-69, 73-74, 80, 82, 88-89, 90, 92-103

A Different Way in Altogether

You may prefer a more multimodal approach but are still interested in what the book and the conversations based on it have to offer you. The book has a wealth of supplementary material in the form of an open-access ETHER Resource Library (accessed via https://ether.leeds .ac.uk/ether-resource-library/). You might, for instance, wish to consider a fuller context of the original contributions from which the book material has been compiled. You can access a full bank of recorded keynotes, conversationist interventions and original provocation videos produced by individual authors on which the conversations represented in this book are based.

If you wish to start with a shorter and a more visual summary of key ideas, you can find these in relevant issues of ETHER News https://ether .leeds.ac.uk/ether-resource-library/ether-newsletters/, each focusing on individual seminars and its primary contributors listed below.

Dearden, L. (2021) *ETHER News 3* (Seminar 1: The Arts of Seeing and Hearing the Other; Dyck, Herxheimer, Mason, Jaffer, Gumede, Finch, Pitman, Shetty, Bock, Krause-Alzaidi, Kent, Beiler, Dewilde, Kelz, Fischer, Jedlinsky, Deumert).

Dearden, L. (2022) *ETHER News 5* (Seminar 2: Ethical Drama of Encountering the Other; Adami, Ahmed, Assaf, Harrington, Blackledge, Creese, Boldt, Valente, Fellows, Jassat, Rapport, Si'ilata, Williams, Einarsson).

Dearden, L. (2022) *ETHER News 7* (Seminar 3: Creating Spaces for Encountering Difference; Youssef, Dove, Khadijah Ibrahim, Awad Ibrahim, Selim, Galloway Gallego, Costley, Reilly, Heidt, Forsdick, Dearden, Douglas, Biesta, Moriarty Harrelson).

Parts of this book are also accompanied by video essays/podcasts with an additional guiding narrative: https://ether.leeds.ac.uk/ether-resource-library/ether-podcast-series/.

Shetty, P. and Kubanyiova, M. (2021) ETHER Podcast: Curating difference for collective action.

Shetty, P. and Kubanyiova, M. (2022a) ETHER Podcast: Encountering through storytelling: Whose listening?

Shetty, P. and Kubanyiova, M. (2022b) ETHER Podcast: Encountering through storytelling: Whose stories?

Shetty, P. and Kubanyiova, M. (2022c) ETHER Podcast: Encountering through storytelling: Whose tellings?

For any practitioners wishing to access examples of teaching materials based on the conversations in this book, you can view a resource for secondary school teachers produced by Izzy Bartley on behalf of Leeds Museums and Galleries and in collaboration with ETHER. These are hosted by MyLearning.org: Free Learning Resources from Arts, Cultural and Heritage Organisations.

Bartley, I., Leeds Museums and Galleries and University of Leeds (2022) Teachers' notes on encountering the other: Discussing identity, difference and belonging. See https://mylearning.org/stories/encountering-the-other/1587.

How We Worked

This book is the outcome of a collaborative endeavour. In addition to us, the editors, the ETHER team included Angela Creese (co-investigator), Louise Dearden and Ana Korzun (project assistants) who all made a direct contribution to the project's content and processes. Additionally, Louise and Ana produced full transcripts of all the ETHER conversations we worked with for this book and some of the supplementary multimodal material we refer to above. All named authors listed in the frontmatter have contributed to the exchange and therefore co-authored this conversation and co-shaped our collective listening. This is regardless of whether or not difficult editorial decisions allowed for their fuller contributions to feature in these pages. We, Maggie Kubanyiova (ETHER principal investigator) and Parinita Shetty (ETHER project assistant and administrator), take full responsibility for re-presenting this knowledge and for any omissions or tunnel visions that inevitably come with our personal biographies, disciplinary training or space limitations. *Listening Without Borders* remains, however, a firm commitment informing our editorial work.

The book features a range of conversations that took place over the course of ETHER. This includes 30 provocations (polemics as blogs and video presentations that participants submitted prior to each seminar and which are available in the public domain at https://ether.leeds.ac.uk/ether -resource-library/519-2/), 15 conversations that the randomly paired-up provocation authors were invited to have with each other, and a range of other forms of dialogue (including dedicated conversation sessions led by appointed conversationists, keynote speeches followed by a Q&A and the parallel chat box that included comments, questions, musings and mini-conversations among ETHER participants).

In addition to the whole-team post-seminar briefings, we made detailed notes on each seminar and held regular team meetings throughout the project to discuss themes that resonated with each of us. As editors, we relistened to the entire recorded material several times, reread and annotated transcripts and brought our observations to regular editorial meetings. Specific issues were repeatedly invoked across the seminars. Similarly, in our ears, different contributions started to speak to each other around larger themes even if the actual exchange never happened in the same timespace. These larger themes eventually became our organising framework and, at the same time, shaped our ethical agency when making difficult editorial decisions about what to include, what to exclude and how to order to practice what we preach within the confines of a short book.

We adhered to several core principles to accomplish the task. Staying open to the polyphony of voices in order to preserve the difference of each contributor's perspective was a key stance that has guided the listening behind our editorial work. Our aim for the book was to create a space of possibility to dwell in the presence of others ethically: without judging, categorising, patronising, dismissing or explaining the other. We brought an anthropological sensibility to our work that orients to participants' perspectives, contextualises them in the settings of their original practice or research and puts them in a larger conversation with each other around common themes. This has resulted in an attentively (or so we hope) re-presented mosaic of ideas rather than a replication of what was said and in the order in which it was said. The fragmented and multimodal format aims to highlight the different kinds of interacting and thinking that emerged while, at the same time, resisting the urge to make the reader too comfortable. As soon as the text gives the appearance of an answer, it throws the reader back into the flow. Finally, each contributor has had multiple opportunities to feed back. Everyone had access to the full manuscript with an opportunity to make any changes they wished. We respected the right of everyone to refuse participation in the book project and acted on any requests to withdraw part or entire contributions. We have also done our best to address constructive feedback received from authors in two rounds of feedback workshops. Any omissions or mistakes remain ours.

No Conclusion?

As we have reiterated several times now, attentive re-presenting of conversations under relevant themes is as far as our interpretation in this book goes. The following pages do not feature any further layered analyses or theoretical narration. Just as our diverse group of participants brought their multiple priorities, interests and perspectives into the space, we want this book to perform a similar function for the reader. How do these ideas speak to you? How or why do they matter in your research, arts or community practice? How do you negotiate difference? In what way does your setting invite, enable or present a possibility for listening without borders?

And yet, we clearly cannot and do not wish to attempt to remove ourselves from the process. We can only present what *we* heard and what *we* have been taught through our listening. Someone else would have produced a different book from the same material. Admittedly, it is also hard to imagine how a book can fulfil its vision as pedagogy for social action without any sort of takeaway of what one should do. There is, then, a conclusion to which we will happily subscribe. The act of participation in the polyphonic flow is the pedagogy (cf. Shetty, 2022), for it can generate moments of being taught (Biesta, 2022). Through our editorial listening, we have experienced and continue to experience many such educational moments. It's rather like 'listening to a train'. We point you to specific juxtapositions because we saw them as meaningful at the time of listening, but do not prescribe what you should hear in them. We do not set borders on your moments of being taught in the presence of these particular others. The connection is yours to make.

References

Bartley, I., Leeds Museums and Galleries and University of Leeds (2022) Teachers' notes on encountering the other: Discussing identity, difference and belonging. See https://mylearning.org/stories/encountering-the-other/1587.
Bassel, L. (2017) *The Politics of Listening: Possibilities and Challenges for Democratic Life*. Palgrave Macmillan.

Biesta, G. (2022) *World-Centred Education: A View for the Present*. Routledge.
Brizić, K. (2024) Unsettled hearing, responsible listening: Encounters with voice after forced migration. *Applied Linguistics Review*. https://doi.org/10.1515/applirev-2024-0088
Connor, J.E. (2023) Hearing the quiet voices: Listening as democratic action in a Norwegian neighborhood. *Language in Society*. https://doi.org/10.1017=S0047404522000677
Davis, M. (1969) Miles Davis interview with Les Tomkins. *National Jazz Archive*. See https://nationaljazzarchive.org.uk/explore/interviews/1633602-miles-davis.
Dearden, L. (2021) *ETHER News 3*. See https://ether.leeds.ac.uk/ether-resource-library/ether-newsletters/.
Dearden, L. (2022a) *ETHER News 5*. See https://ether.leeds.ac.uk/ether-resource-library/ether-newsletters/.
Dearden, L. (2022b) *ETHER News 7*. See https://ether.leeds.ac.uk/ether-resource-library/ether-newsletters/.
Hall, S. (2007) Living with difference: Stuart Hall in conversation with Bill Schwarz. *Soundings: A Journal of Politics and Culture* 37 (Winter), 148–158. See https://journals.lwbooks.co.uk/soundings/vol-2007-issue-37/article-7152/
Inoue, M. (2003) The listening subject of Japanese modernity and his auditory double: Citing, sighting, and siting the modern Japanese woman. *Cultural Anthropology* 18 (2), 156–193.
Krause-Alzaidi, L.-S. (2024) Becoming responsible with a protest placard: White under(-)standing in encounters with the Black German Other. *Applied Linguistics Review*. https://doi.org/10.1515/applirev-2024-0087
Kubanyiova, M. (2024) (Im)possibility of ethical encounters in places of separation: Towards aesthetics as a quiet applied linguistics research praxis. *Applied Linguistics Review*. https://doi.org/10.1515/applirev-2024-0082
Lillie, J. and Larsen, K. (eds) (2024) *The Relationship is the Project*. NewSouth Publishing.
McKemey, M.B., Rangers, B., Rangers, Y.M., Costello, O., Hunter, J.T. and Ens, E.J. (2022) 'Right-way' science: Reflections on co-developing Indigenous and Western cross-cultural knowledge to support Indigenous cultural fire management. *Ecological Management & Restoration* 23 (S1), 75–82.
Robertson, P. (2016) *Soundscapes: A Musician's Journey through Life and Death*. Faber & Faber.
Rosa, J. (2019) *Looking Like a Language, Sounding Like a Race: Raciolinguistic Ideologies and the Learning of Latinidad*. Oxford University Press.
Shetty, P. (2022) Marginally fannish: Fan podcasts as sites of public pedagogy and intersectional education. Doctoral dissertation, University of Leeds.
Shetty, P. and Kubanyiova, M. (2021) ETHER podcast: Curating difference for collective action. See https://ether.leeds.ac.uk/ether-resource-library/ether-podcast-series/.
Shetty, P. and Kubanyiova, M. (2022a) ETHER podcast: Encountering through storytelling: Whose listening? See https://ether.leeds.ac.uk/ether-resource-library/ether-podcast-series/.
Shetty, P. and Kubanyiova, M. (2022b) ETHER podcast: Encountering through storytelling: Whose stories? See https://ether.leeds.ac.uk/ether-resource-library/ether-podcast-series/.
Shetty, P. and Kubanyiova, M. (2022c) ETHER podcast: Encountering through storytelling: Whose tellings? See https://ether.leeds.ac.uk/ether-resource-library/ether-podcast-series/.
Smith, Z. (2022) Somebody in here after all: Introduction to Toni Morrison's Recitatif. In T. Morrison (auth) *Recitatif* (pp. vii–xlv). Chatto & Windus.
Snell, J. and Cushing, I. (2022) 'A lot of them write how they speak': Policy, pedagogy and the policing of 'nonstandard' English. *Literacy* 56 (3), 199–211.
Williams, Q. (2024) Towards a sociolinguistics of in difference: Stancetaking on others. *Applied Linguistics Review*. https://doi.org/10.1515/applirev-2024-0090.

2 Communicating Within, Between and Beyond Social Categories

Butcher's window in Kirkgate market (Elisabetta Adami, 2017)

Dwelling Inside, Dwelling Outside

Charlotta Palmstierna Einarsson

The ETHER (Ethics and Aesthetics of Encountering the Other) project's overarching question 'How do people of conflicting worldviews, memories and future visions encounter each other?' seems to target Dan Zahavi's claim that 'the capacity to engage in different types of collective intentionality is often considered a key feature in human sociality'.[1] Notably, as Sahavi points out, the relation between we and I is not merely a theoretical question but one with tangible practical effects that we experience on a daily basis. As human beings, we are friends or foes, club members, butterfly collectors, academics, lovers, neurotics, heterosexual, homo, transgender or cis persons, conservative, liberal, feminists, young, middle-aged, old or dog lovers. The list goes on. And if prompted to define who we are, we reach for criteria to justify our belonging to certain communities that are directed at certain ideas, activities or values. That is, our sense of belonging to community predicates on what Dan Sahavi calls collective intentionality.

Identity on this spectrum is intersectional as Kimberlé Williams Crenshaw pointed out in 1989.[2] There are certain aspects of a person's identity that tend to be privileged over others. And the issue of how we negotiate our inclusion in or exclusion from communities of speakers is therefore a matter of participation and thus intrinsically ethical. Difference conceived, for instance in terms of collective intentionality, emerged from discourse, and the context in which communication takes place could be seen to regulate such differentiating processes.

In preparing for this talk, I began by imagining a community of like-minded individuals – an assumption that brought the 'we' to mind. Based on my understanding of the significance of the overarching question that ETHER asks, I also imagined this community could be keenly sensitive to the subtle workings of power, to the processes by which issues of power frame human interaction, and to the ethics of acknowledging this situation. Yet, in so doing, I was immediately reminded of Timothy Garton Ash's thought-provoking question: 'When you say we, who do you mean? What's the widest possible political community of which you spontaneously say "we" or "us"?'[3]

In our answer to that question, Garton Ash points out, lies the key to our future.

As Garton Ash's question suggests, then, the notion of we is inevitably divided along philosophical, social and political lines. And trying to answer it, I realised that I had to call my own assumptions about belonging to community into question; not because I believed I was wrong in envisioning a group of like-minded individuals interested in the ethics of communicating with the other, but because I realised that I could not clearly specify the nature of the we I had in mind.

> I understand that I will never understand but I stand with you.

Lara-Stephanie Krause-Alzaidi

In encounters in Germany there are apparatuses[4] at work that constantly measure for blackness but not for whiteness. So these apparatuses – of which I am a part – actually enact cuts that produce black bodies and German bodies, but not white bodies. Because white bodies and German bodies are conflated, no cuts are being enacted there. Only between German bodies and black bodies. Currently, white Germans are not a thing because they are *the* thing. So, what does that mean for us? Well, I would say that this means that participation in material discursive practices which enact cuts that produce white Germans and black Germans might actually be our responsibility.

So, let me get back to the Black Lives Matter (BLM) slogans and what we can learn from them in this regard and also with this theoretical lens. In an interview with Noëmi, a black German woman, we were looking at and talking about a selection of BLM protest placards that I had compiled on a PowerPoint slide. While Noëmi knew that what brought me into this research had been this placard: 'I understand that I will never understand but I stand with you', she started talking about all the other slogans I presented but she didn't really talk about this one. And I said, 'Well you've ignored this one so far so let's look at it'. And she said, 'Yeah that was easy for me to ignore that poster because for me it's essentially a poster that if we're talking about Black Lives Matter protests, it must and should only be brought and carried by white people or by people who are read as white'.

So, we can see here, with Noëmi's help, the enaction of difference as cutting together apart: there's a cut being enacted here between white people or white bodies who would be the ones forming assemblages with this particular slogan. Word–body–assemblages – or placard–body–unions – enact a cut between them and black bodies within the BLM movement. But then Noëmi goes on immediately to say, 'Well I would love to take the poster with me if I went to protest against trans- or homophobia, for example. So say I go somewhere where I stand in for trans rights, then I can put myself in those shoes and take on the perspective that maybe a white person would have at a Black Lives Matter protest'. So, thinking through these 'word–body–assemblages' – which enact cuts that differentiate and connect in one move – opens up new possibilities for making relations, showing solidarity, identifying with each other.

> We use collective terms for anyone that isn't white and this reduces our individuality to an acronym and it kind of dispels any sort of freedom and inclusivity that we need to feel accepted.

Mohasin Ahmed

In modern-day Western society, visibility and equality have improved for our communities. Equality legislation means that Queer people and People of Colour (PoC) have more equal opportunities and see themselves represented in society better. So why, in 2021, is a space like Mojxmma, a club night for Queer People of Colour, needed? Something that demonstrates this need is the 'Progress Pride flag', which was created in 2017 by American civil rights activist Amber Hikes in direct response to the racial discrimination that Queer People of Colour were facing in gay bars in Philadelphia. This experience is not exclusive to Philadelphia. I myself did not feel comfortable as a Queer femme and as a person of Colour in the majority of Queer spaces that I entered. These clubs catered for the majority within the minority and that is White cisgender, homosexual men. You can assume that when you go to a gay bar that there will not be any homophobia but you can't assume that there will not be any racism/transphobia/sexism.

It may be a surprise that discrimination exists within our community but it is a common experience, illustrated in a survey by Stonewall UK in 2018, which found that 51% of LGBT Black, Asian and minority ethnic (BAME) respondents had experienced racism within the community. This increased to 61% for Black LGBT people specifically. Disabled people as a group with pre-existing barriers to support and inclusion also face discrimination within the community and LGBT clubs and events are often not catered for them, dividing the community further. Bisexual people are often dismissed as heterosexual or 'still in the closet'. Some people do not accept them as part of the community as they can 'pass' as straight and might not face the same struggles as homosexual people if in a heterosexual relationship. Transgender people also face discrimination within the community by those who do not believe that they should be included in the LGBT+ spectrum. An example of this is the LGB Alliance, a registered charity in the UK, which actively promotes trans-exclusionary rhetoric.

This brings me to the theory of intersectionality. This was introduced by Kimberlé Crenshaw in 1989 to explain how different aspects of identity can intersect and compound discrimination. Crenshaw's initial example was using the intersection of race and gender to illustrate the unique experience of Black women in America. During the feminist and anti-racist movements of that period, Crenshaw argues that Black women were left behind by a White-centric model of feminism and a male-centric model of racism. Furthermore, the experience of discrimination faced by Black women that is rooted in both racism and misogyny is ignored, causing significant numbers of people in our communities to be underserved by social justice frames because they don't address the particular ways that they're experiencing discrimination.

We can see examples of these intersections within the LGBT community. People with intersecting identities often code switch, masking parts of their identity to be accepted in specific spaces. We, as others, encounter those outside of our community by shape-shifting to what we feel is acceptable in that space. I think that recognising intersectional identities is the most important point. We are all multidimensional – we have our ethnicity, culture, religion, gender, sexuality, experiences, personality and stories. When providing spaces to include others, we must realise that we all have different needs. The 'others' are usually lumped together; we say the LGBT+ community for all gender and sexuality spectrums that are not cisgender or heterosexual, and BAME/PoC, for all ethnicities that are non-White, ignoring the rich culture, religion, beliefs and experiences that each group hold.

> While the disappearance of this cultural capital is evident, visual arts presents the possibility for reimagining schools through approaches that validate Pasifika perspectives.

Dagmar Dyck

> Tēnā koutou katoa
> *Greetings to you all*
> He uri tēnei no ngā whenua o Tonga, no Hamene
> *My ancestors come from Tonga and Germany*
> E noho ana au kei Tāmaki Makaurau
> *I live in the city of Auckland*
> He ringa toi au, otirā ko au te kaiwhakahaere hōtaka o te
> matauranga Pasifika – Uniservices kei te Waipapa Taumata Rau
> *I am an artist as well as the programme manager for Pacific-*
> *led Education – Uniservices at the University of Auckland.*
> Ko Dagmar Dyck tōku ingoa
> *My name is Dagmar Dyck*
> Tēnā tātou
> *Greetings to us all*

I am a first-generation New Zealander living and working in our largest city Tāmaki Makaurau, Auckland. My mother is German Tongan from Vava'u, Tonga, and my father is German Polish Dutch.

My entire life I have felt my difference. I look different to the dominant culture, my name Dagmar Dyck sounds different, my parents speak different languages, our family traditions are different. Being different is part of the framework of my identity.

In our sea of islands, Tongan scholar Epeli Hau'ofa[5] writes, 'Whatever we produce must not be a version of our existing reality, which is largely a creation of imperialism. It must be different and of our own making. We should not forget that human reality is human creation. If we fail to create our own, someone else will do it for us by default'. Hau'ofa believed in an individual's right to be custodians of their own knowledge and identity so that their realities are not only learned and understood but also shared.

As a Pasifika artist, social justice activist and art educator, I believe that the arts and storytelling are powerful levers for those like myself where being different is our lived experience. Arts and storytelling are interlinked in the way that we as Pacific peoples create our arts and provide the vā or spaces in which we tell them.

My difference plays a fundamental role in the way I navigate my world. Throughout my schooling years, I never had a teacher or lecturer who reflected me, nor did I have conversations with teachers about my exact identity, an experience that made me feel culturally invisible. However, through the deliberate actions of my art teachers, they recognised the creative capacity in me. They encouraged me to use my art as a platform and vehicle to tell my story. The rest is history.

New Zealand's education system has generally remained silent on the topic of whiteness, white privilege and supremacy and the Eurocentric nature of our schooling policy and practice.[6] Relevant to New Zealand-born Pasifika students and families is the acknowledgement of language and culture loss as a result of colonisation. While the disappearance of this cultural capital is evident, the visual arts presents the possibility for reimagining schools through approaches that validate Pasifika perspectives.

Social Standing I and II (Original artwork; Dagmar Dyck, 2023; photo by Sam Hartnett)

> Not being able to attune to one another not only means fail-
> ing to communicate with the other, it could also mean shut-
> ting people down.

Erin Moriarty

Turning to Washington, DC, these are photos of my neighbourhood. Public spaces in DC were radically transformed and everyday encounters became fraught as a result of tumultuous events on the Capitol throughout the Trump administration. I live on Capitol Hill, a few blocks from the Capitol, where Congress meets and the epicentre for encounters between US citizens and their representatives. During lockdown, I would take daily walks to the Capitol. On and off, the Capitol and its surrounding blocks had been fenced off from ordinary citizens because of the protests that had been taking place in the neighbourhood on a daily basis.

A person dressed in a red, hooded robe in Washington DC (Erin Moriarty, 2021)

On this particular day, the tall fences had been taken down and only a few barriers remained. In front of the barriers, I encountered a person dressed in a red, hooded robe, standing with their head bowed. There was a powerful stillness, as this woman was a solitary figure standing in front of the barriers surrounding an empty expanse of concrete in front of one of the most powerful symbols of American democracy. This person stood there, in the shimmering heat, silently resisting the former president and the direction he was taking the country in. The photo is from 2020, and her red robe was redolent of the book and the television series *The Handmaid's Tale*. This encounter was with a lone figure, head bowed in silent protest, in a landscape of stillness, as we were the only two people there, besides the figures on the steps of the Capitol in all black with machine guns. The aesthetics of the moment did not invite conversation. However, as I encountered her in the stillness in front of the Capitol, I became witness to her silent protest.

Awad Ibrahim

For Buber,[7] language or, more broadly, communication is central to any form of dialogue, even though dialogue can take place in silence. To be able to communicate in silence is the human capacity that he calls communicating inter-subjectively. This kind of communication happens outside language and outside the speech act. And so, even though dialogue can exist outside the boundaries of language and in silence, communication is, nonetheless, an essential component of dialogue. As an event, dialogue is deeply embedded in time and space. For dialogue to take place, especially what he calls 'genuine dialogue', requires a quality of communication that he calls communion. A sense of time, place and, above all, a sense of recognising the humanity of the other. This means moving from a simple dialogue to becoming an act of love.

Ana Deumert

Angela, when you mentioned the word moral, for me it's interesting because you then mentioned ethics as well. And somehow ethics is a word I feel quite comfortable with. To me, moral immediately evokes the moralistic, the self-righteousness. I think that's why, very often, we tend to – I tend to – prefer the word ethics because it doesn't seem to have those connotations of somebody judging someone; whereas moral seems, to me at least, to somehow have that implication, including the negative associations of being moralistic.

Angela Creese

Yeah, I agree with you, I think it does. Although having now read some of the literature which I wasn't engaging with before, I can see that it is much more about responsibility. And the dynamic that's created in the relational with people being together is a kind of moral responsibility. So, I think it's a bit like the word individuality as well – it means very different things to different people obviously.

The thing about ethics though is that it's too easily linked these days with a kind of ethical form filling and going through the university systems. That takes on another dimension of meaning. In sociolinguistics it's also an issue because when we talk about interaction, we're very much at ease going into meaning and indexicality and other processes of meaning making. But we still find it very hard to talk about the ethical or moral dimension of interacting with one another. And I think that's one of the things I've learned from Maggie asking me questions about my work. I know we're not all sociolinguists, but this is a point where I find this really speaks to me. I want to be able to bring in a different dimension of interaction that is much harder for a linguist to do.

Elisabetta Adami

I will bring a couple of examples of meaning-making towards a perceived other done by using objects as resources of communication. These examples will lead me to ask questions on appropriation and on what defines successful communication. I will not provide answers but rather try to show how, by looking at instances of communication beyond language, we might be able to uncover principles and practices of meaning making with 'perceived others' that help us dismantle ideas of 'intercultural' as hinged on national or ethnic criteria and, possibly, redefine 'otherness' and 'kin' in more dynamic, relational, situated and emerging ways.

Sociolinguistics and applied linguistic research on language, culture and intercultural communication has long advocated against an essentialised conception of culture based on national or ethnic boundaries. However, intra-linguistic and inter-linguistic contexts are still considered as separate. That is, while communication among people with different mother tongues would be considered in the realm of intercultural communication, communication among people with the same mother tongue and possibly using different varieties would be considered in the realm of societal power dynamics instead, not within intercultural communication. When, in reality, I argue that both contexts should always fall within the same case of communication with perceived others.

Now, although I'm a linguist, I'm particularly interested in meaning made by so-called non-verbal resources and how the meaning-making principles that are in place when we use these resources with perceived others might shed new light on concepts of culture, communication and possibly also on how we use speech and writing in this context.

So, I'll use one example of this through the use of objects in a public space and specifically in the window of a butcher in Kirkgate Market in Leeds City Centre (see image at the beginning of this chapter). And this is one of the findings that emerged during a three-year project that I worked on with other colleagues in Leeds; the project was funded by the British Academy and the Leverhulme Trust. It was called 'Leeds Voices – Communicating Superdiversity in the Market'.

Now, this butcher has placed a lucky cat in his shop window close to where he displays belly pork. He has done that to attract Chinese customers, because in his experience Chinese customers frequently buy belly pork unlike other customer demographics. So here, he has used an object as a resource, he has turned it into a sign that, in its intended meaning, addresses Chinese customers – it says 'you' Chinese customers – and indexically, through proximity placement, draws their attention to an item that they might want to buy.

From this example, we can ask many questions. Is the sign successful? What does it mean for a sign to be successful? Is it a case of cultural appropriation? We could certainly ask Chinese customers passing by what meaning they make of the lucky cat. And most likely we'll receive very many different answers.

But that's not really my point. When I came across that shop window, I had recently arrived in the UK, the Brexit referendum results had just been released and I started to feel particularly conscious of the popularity of an anti-immigration stance blowing across this island. The butcher also has a Union Jack outside his window. And that's used to show the provenance of its activity and produce. But within the Brexit climate, I have become more and more triggered to interpret UK national flags on display as a nationalistic sign potentially associated with anti-immigration ideas.

So, in this case, as a recently arrived migrant, I interpreted the lucky cat as a sign of openness towards foreignness, mitigating the potentially nationalistic and neo-nativist meaning that I would associate with the Union Jack on display. Although the lucky cat did not mean to me what the butcher intended it to mean, it was indeed successful. It let me enter without fear. Not in indexing the belly pork, which I didn't even notice, but rather in pre-empting a potential meaning of 'I don't welcome migrants'.

There is more, because in the very same window, the butcher has also placed some plastic grapes on display. He did that when fishmongers were temporarily relocated to the butcher's aisle when their hall in the market was undergoing renovation. Traditionally, fishmongers have a higher-budget clientele than butchers in the market. The butcher told me that he thought he needed to decorate his window, given the many 'posh' customers now walking down his aisle. So, he's used plastic grapes. In this case again he used a resource that he thought would appeal to the taste (that is, would speak the register) of a perceived other – not in nationality, as with Chinese customers for the lucky cat, but rather in class this time – people with a 'higher taste' if you will. Here again, was this an intended cultural appropriation, even if it ended up using a resource that does not belong to the intended addressed audience? But also, was the sign successful? Most likely 'posh' customers would interpret the plastic grapes as a sign of 'authenticity' (not certainly belonging to their taste, but belonging to a somewhat 'inferior' other, which is endowed with some fascination). The principle is one of 'exoticising', not in nationality but in class in this case.

Now, had he done all this with language, he'd have had to use Chinese to address Chinese customers for the belly pork – thus failing to communicate to me as I can't read Chinese – and some sort of English hypercorrection in place of the plastic grapes to address the posh customers – which would have exposed him to judgments of being illiterate instead of being 'authentic'. Most importantly, with language it would have been difficult to identify these two cases as being the result of the same meaning-making principle, that is, to address – to reach out to – a perceived other by using the resources that are perceived to belong to them.

My provocation to you would be then: What if we looked at meaning-making with the other starting from what we do with signs beyond language, considering that these have not undergone the same level of national codification? Could we possibly have a glimpse of different interpretive paradigms on how we communicate with others – and even more so on the dynamics that lead each of us to perceive somebody as other or as kin?

Charlotta Palmstierna Einarsson

According to Gendlin, we are not self-sufficient autonomous subjects but we are interaction. Gendlin's process model of thinking opens up a route for thinking about the distinctions between self and other based on the role of the body in experience.[8,9]

In Gendlin's account, then, humans are embodied interaction; the motive being that, again according to Schoeller and Dunaetz, it could be more fruitfully understood in terms of kung fu or dance.[10] In kung fu, they explain, one learns to absorb the energy of the other as part of striking back or shifting direction. The point is that human beings are not entities that somehow interact, but that our notions of subjectivity and identity emerge from interaction.

As a former dancer, I confess to being particularly attuned to this description. In my experience, to dance is to interact – with spatial orientations, for instance, the corner of a room or the floor – and to do so in ways that seem to produce a form of time-space mattering that Karen Barad associates with entanglements.[11] To dance is to absorb and produce weight, orientation, rhythm and shape. And these material phenomena emerge only through being entangled in this particular way. By analogy, musicians performing a piece do not play alongside each other but they attune to each other and music emerges from their musical entanglements.

The emphasis on embodied cognition does not deny the significance of language. It only insists that we rethink our processes of sense-making. Attuning to embodied cognition arguably reveals our mode of being in the world as intrinsically incomplete. We cannot create meaning on our own, says Gendlin, nor can we speak a private language, says Wittgenstein, but we emerge from interaction as do meanings, concepts and identities.[12] Attunement to embodied cognition is therefore an important potential resource for thinking and for communicating with the other. According to Gabriel Carter, the reason why the idea of attunement is so important in new materialism is precisely that it emphasises the intrinsic interconnections between self and other, human and non-human, subject and object – and that it does so in a way that is rhetorical. As Carter suggests, quoting Lydia Walsh, an inability to attune is a rhetorical failing.[13]

Even more specifically, he explains, 'attunement offers the individual entangled within an assemblage a practice; not a task with which one could complete but an ongoing practice of interrogating one's own complicit participation via their practices in the becoming of an assemblage'. Basically, we must attune or fail. And not being able to attune not only means failing to communicate with the other, but it could also mean shutting people down.

To be attuned, then, is to participate and share in the production of meaning. And as Jane Bennett explains, this is also to participate in the ongoing creative processes that constitute various modes of 'being towards others'.[14] As such, one could say that it also approaches what Richard Kearney terms being towards others, a mode of being that 'in itself is an ethical gesture of welcoming what is different'.[15] In making claims, we are thus appealing to others to share in our understanding of the world, to see our reason and commitment to certain values. And the wider the context we can imagine for our claims, the more universal they seem to be; and the more universal, the truer they also seem to be.

Interrupting Assumptions

> When you begin to name differences as cultural differences, you'll begin to explain them. And those explanations actually remove you from the encounter.

Gert Biesta

In relation to the question of culture, and again in the whole field of intercultural communication and cultural education, many scholars have raised a really important and valuable question about culture. Can we simply map nation onto culture onto language? Of course not. Can we think of culture as monolithic and static? Of course not. Can we simply say that identity is linked with culture and becomes cultural identity? Also not.

But, again, one question that I see less there, but maybe it says something about my reading, is that these discussions sort of assume that culture exists. And I'm always inclined to say culture is not a thing. Culture is a very particular explanation of the experience of difference. You could even say that culture is an explanation of encounter. But culture is never the encounter itself. The problem is that when you use the word culture, very quickly you work with the distinction of nature and culture. And then when you begin to name differences as cultural differences, I think you begin to explain them in a very particular way. And my worry is that those explanations actually eradicate the difference. They remove you from the encounter. So, to say to someone else, your difference from me is merely cultural, we're actually saying, it appears as cultural within the frame I have, and there is no longer the question of whether that frame itself is shared. That's why a lot of the social cultural theories going around in education for me are problematic.

And you can also say that when culture appears as an explanation for difference, it has a really colonial gesture in it where you say, I claim the right to explain you from where I am.

Now, when we think of these encounters as intercultural encounters, you can say that these encounters are framed in a very particular way, which I would characterise as viewing the other. That means that in that understanding of intercultural relationships and encounters, you can say that I am positioned as a spectator of the other. I like the German word Beobachter. When you have this image and begin to think back about all these competency frameworks for intercultural communication, what they all try to do is to see how I can become more competent as a spectator of others. And I think that's a problematic way of staging what's going on.

The problem is that in one and the same move, the 'I' only arrives in the world as a spectator, as a viewer. And this, I think, is still troubling a lot of talk and understanding about intercultural encounters, encounters with the other; that they always start with an 'I' who then needs to encounter, connect, understand, empathise with, get into a dialogue.

Here I see the importance of the work of Emmanuel Levinas which has also come up in the ETHER project because Levinas, in a sense, raises a very fundamental question about what he calls an ego logical worldview, a worldview that starts with the ego, and assumes the ego is there first and then the ego begins to engage with the world, with other people, with living nature. Levinas pushes back against that idea and I think that's a helpful response. He pushes back against the idea that we first need to know before we can act, pushes back against the idea that we first need to understand before we can live, you could say. So, in a slightly bigger way of putting it, he pushes back against any idea that a theoretical perspective on the world comes first, that I am there first and have a view of the world, and then everything else begins.

Ingrid Rodrick Beiler and *Joke Dewilde*

We knew we were doing something wrong when our potential participants reacted to our consent form as if it were a summons from the secret police. We eventually realised that we were dealing with differences not only of language and educational background but also of biography and memory.

Our current context of research consists of three classes for migrant learners considered to have little formal schooling, at an adult education centre in Norway. Here, we interpret difference to refer to biographical difference, especially in terms of memories of governance and communication. Several learners have lived in Afghanistan, Eritrea, Iraq or Syria, where they have had negative experiences, including bad memories of encounters with the government. We have noted that their linguistic repertoires intersect with these memories in complex ways. These kinds of biographies do not mesh easily with what is expected from researchers who are required to follow the Norwegian research ethics regime.

Research in Norway is subject to one of the strictest regulatory regimes in Europe. Since the implementation of the General Data Protection Regulation, the national regulatory body for research ethics has required the use of an extended template for project information and participant consent. Given the differences in language and literacy among our potential participants, we were mindful of the need to adapt and go beyond macroethical procedures.[16] However, even after simplification, written translation and oral explanation in learners' most proficient languages, a surprisingly large number refused to participate.

To better understand the reasons for the learners' scepticism, we deferred more to the judgment of others – teachers, translators and research assistants – than we had done in previous research. The following excerpt from an interview with Zahra, a multilingual teacher at the school, points to troubling associations with formal letters for some learners:

Zahra:	Yes it was those forms like consent forms, I think that was very difficult for the learners, the translation was a bit, bit too difficult for them to understand, so I thought that maybe that could be a little simpler, in a way, don't write so much about everything, everything you do, it would have been a little easier just to write a little, how we will protect you, how we will protect the (xxxx), so that was a little too much for them.
Joke:	Right, we'll do that, we will raise that, because we're required to use those specific forms, but uh, it is, I completely agree with you that it became too difficult and that, we didn't manage to communicate well enough to the learners what it was really about [...]
Zahra:	And then there are many of them who are traumatised, they have, many of them have internal traumas, so when they hear those kinds of words, then the anxiety comes, then it's best

to use very simple language, because in homeland, like in Iraq when we use that kind of language that's in the form in Arabic, the only thing we have heard of is when there was a letter from the police or from- from- when someone is going to jail, so then that- that is what was, was a bit difficult for them.

Joke: Are you thinking that, for another time, we should just have had the forms in Norwegian and had for example a person like you explain in the mother tongue and that they then sign in Norwegian?

Zahra: Yes, I think so, I think it would make it a bit easier.

In a similar vein, some learners specifically did not want us to take field notes while observing, as this evoked memories of the police taking notes for surveillance or during interrogation. This surprised us, as we expected learners to find field notes to be less invasive than recording.[17] Furthermore, the teachers reported that many learners were concerned that we came from the university to check on their teachers because they were not doing their job well. The teachers had to reassure them that this was a collaborative research project that they had welcomed.

Increasingly, we looked at the consent process in terms of not just satisfying a requirement, but also considering it as data of how differences encounter one another, producing unpredictable outcomes. It required us to ask how we as researchers could better understand participants. Reflexivity and monitoring the process of research took us into researching 'engagement with difference' and discovering what kind of difference we have to negotiate and what effort this takes, in terms of both time and meaning making.

> The hardest part about doing this kind of work is that the ground beneath is not settled. And the moment it becomes settled, then we really need to start to attend to the fact that we're not opening ourselves to the possibilities of difference.

Joseph Valente

I like what you're saying about not making a claim because it's like when we were writing about the non-verbal child in that preschool in Paris and how we argued that we could not make claims about what his actions meant. We talked about the productiveness for us to think about his difference and the way it affected us and the productiveness of the fact that we didn't know what he really thought or what it meant to him. So, if you're doing this kind of work, you can't make claims, right?

Gail Boldt

I mean it's not possible for us not to make claims. I make claims all the time because I have to have a method for working so I have to have some way of thinking about the fact that I do this or I don't do that. So, I make claims but I have to hold those claims really lightly.

Joseph Valente

All right, we don't want to hold steadfast to them, we're not rigid about it. Or, at least, we are transparent about the fact that we are making claims, right?

Gail Boldt

They're working hypotheses.

Joseph Valente

It's a process and you're recognising that it's always already becoming, right? The minute you make claims with certainty about it, then you're no longer attending to the possibilities of that potential or the potential of it becoming something other than what you expected. It's like that paper you gave about Wilfred Bion[18] who writes about going into therapy sessions with patients without memory or desire. You have to enter the session without memory or desire but part of that is that it's impossible to enter sessions without memory or desire. So, you hold the impossibility.

Gail Boldt

You hold the impossibility even though it's impossible. You still try, right? Or to see what gets produced and the difference between what's impossible and what you do to hold on to the productiveness of the difference.

Elisabetta Adami

Something that possibly connects with my interests about communicating with others is that I felt both excitement and frustration by watching your provocation. Excitement about getting access to the other's universe that's unfamiliar to me, but also frustration because I constantly try to translate it into my own universe and that's exhausting. And I think that is also the kernel of how I conceive of communicating with others or trying to make meaning of the other in a sense.

What Gail mentioned about the non-making claims, the non-representational in trying to not make claims, not fix the way I interpret things, which I very much agree on. It's also my social semiotic take on meaning making. I'm wondering if that is asignifying or if it is, in fact, meaning making but it's actually rather the need to accept that, even if we are committed to non-making claims, we also need to accept that we keep making hypotheses. We can't help, and rightly so, but make educated guesses and hypotheses and we keep trying to make meaning. And what's important, I would say, is the ability to acknowledge that these are just hypotheses, they are not set in stone definitions. The idea of accepting the fact that you can't have control of others' meaning making but you also can never be in someone else's head. I felt it also as part of my frustration. I wanted to be in your head while you were there co-constructing this dialogue. Instead, I had to accept the fact that I had to make my own meaning out of it.

Gail Boldt

We frustrate ourselves and each other all the time. It does have to do with disruption, actually, of what we imagine we know through our usual modes of communication. And I guess it's that thing of something that you can't say very much about because it can't be said and also holding onto the productive value of knowing that there is all this stuff that we can't say anything about. Also, we are most excited about the productivity of difference. I mean we can't help but make claims. We have to have ways of working and being in the world. But if we can do that and, at the same time, say but this isn't what it is… that certainly leads you to a lifetime of self-frustration.

Joseph Valente

The hardest part about doing this kind of work is that the ground beneath is not settled. And the moment it becomes settled, we really need to start attending to the fact that we're not opening ourselves to the possibilities of difference and variation. But really, if you think about the ideas, what's happening is you have multiplicity, right? Here are multiple things that can happen. And there are multiple sides of the same point at any time you think you're perceiving something, right?

Gail Boldt

I'll pop in one more thing which is, Elisabetta, about the frustration that you felt. Joe and I are frustrated with each other all the time, and part of that is that we're communicating across deaf, non-deaf differences. And so, I guess I'm interested in the productivity of the frustration which really characterises our relationship and the work we try to do all the time.

Maggie Kubanyiova

And a related idea is about how you actually communicate this. I love the idea of interrupting assumptions by using the cartoon, as you, Gail and Joe, did, which made me pause and think about what it is I'm looking at. So, the whole idea of representation and what we're doing, through dance, cartoons or other creative forms of communicating our research, that question always goes back to the ethics of aesthetics. And again, I think I'm alluding to Joe here. So, when we're talking about aesthetics, a way of assembling different forms to represent or communicate, what is the ethics of that? There will always be questions about what right we have to represent. But should we also be concerned with what kind of ethical responsibility we have and what kind of ethical response we want to invite?

Charlotta Palmstierna Einarsson

In terms of that ethical response, I would say that it's very difficult to remember the flow of our ideas, the flow of life. We get so caught up in meanings and we keep taking them for granted. For me, it's very much about interrupting myself to remind myself of that. I don't know if I always succeed; I mean, often I don't succeed. I can look back and say, 'Oh my goodness, I just took that as a given or forgot to listen'. But that's very human to be completely immersed in life and in ideology.

The question is, dare to challenge yourself. I think that may be very difficult, it may be very scary. And that's one way of securing a more ethical stance towards the other: to remember that perhaps you haven't been walking in their shoes; you don't know what kind of life they're leading.

I consider myself really privileged to be able to say what I want in most contexts, not in all contexts. But you don't see your own privilege, you forget about your own privilege. And we have a tendency – and when I say we, I mean human beings – to just see the things that confirm our own understanding of the world as it already is, and it can be really difficult to challenge that.

Quentin Williams

What I want to demonstrate is an analysis of reaction videos towards a parody performance by an emerging pop group called Woman2Woman based in Cape Town who used Coloured English with Kaaps which is understood as a historically racialised variety of Afrikaans. The reaction videos on YouTube show how speakers or YouTube users are invested in language ideological frameworks of *in difference*.

Why reaction videos? Reaction videos are a uniquely YouTube or social media framework because they have transformed the nature of self-imaging platforms such as YouTube and Instagram. It is an important data source to study the performance of language, gender and race and the many ways users provide a multimodal affective experience. According to McDaniel,[19] reaction videos are an effective response to media that generates further engagement because reactivity points to a quality of media that transforms reception into interaction by provoking a response.

Woman2Woman performed a parody of Beyonce Knowles' song *Irreplaceable* on a famous show called Morning Soul Expresso in 2017. They are all so-called Coloured speakers in Cape Town, which is often defined as a racial label that describes not White enough, not Black enough. And on this particular day, they parodied Coloured English together with Kaaps to present a funny rendition of the song which is about Beyonce Knowles breaking up with her boyfriend because presumably he has cheated.

Coloured English becomes embodied in the performance of the parody. Woman2Woman embodied their performance in such a way that they challenged language ideological discourses of *in difference* that attempted to reduce their exaggerated use of Coloured English and Kaaps as inauthentic and erroneous and contradictory. I pay particular attention not only to the group's performance but also to the linguistic hate that resulted from the imposition of language ideologies of *in difference* that came the group's way once their performance was published on YouTube.

A lot of the reactionary comments below the video were filled with sarcasm and mocking but also reflected on the use of English by the participants. The users responded through conjectures and determinations that their performance caused linguistic feuds, confusion and 'how-dare-they perform-that-Beyonce-song-in-that-variety', leading to a fair amount of hate. So, in exaggerating Coloured English alongside Kaaps, users did not provide a very good description but were sarcastic, mocked it and tried to affiliate the use of Coloured English with that of a woman speaking either Indian or the other performers not speaking proper English.

In the reaction to the expression videos, this performance represents language discourses of *in difference* that seek to bind the discourses of race to the group's racialised and gendered bodies and their singing ability; not only their ability to use a certain variety of English, in this case Coloured English and the use of Afrikaans, but also the confusion around its use in the song. In many of the reactions, the users try to figure this out in the song. These metalinguistic reflections of some of the users rely on language ideological discourses of *in difference* as conjecture – seeing the group's use of the type of English and accent as violating standard language norms, that is, standard English language norms.

I interpret this to be language ideologies of *in difference* as tied to discourses of integration of gender and speech in the use of a racialised form of English. I am interested in demonstrating more specifically how one racialised variety of South African English, that is Coloured English, is used and exaggerated by performers and is framed by discourses of *in difference* by other speakers who arrive at language ideologies of *in difference* by conjecture, determinations and contradictions across forms and modes. Through the parody of Coloured English, that is historically racialised varieties, speakers challenge and critique language ideological *in difference* frameworks and they do so because they are often at the vanguard of reinventing language in egalitarian ways.

The Woman2Woman performance is indicative of what happens to previously racialised forms when they are rethought and relinked to voices that challenge language ideologies of *in difference* that are represented through conjectures, determinations and contradictions; and in our case by YouTube users familiar and unfamiliar with the multilingual realities and social, cultural, communication lives of a group like Woman2Woman. By exaggerating Coloured English through parody and the matrices of gender, linguistic power and hegemony, Woman2Woman provides an example of what exactly speakers of historically racialised forms and languages are doing with language inclusivity and recognition.

Lastly, I want to say that Woman2Woman's performance demonstrates that the reappropriation of language by communities of speakers on the periphery often involves and evolves understandings of language authenticity and ownership that divert significantly from more institutionalised discourses on language. And it is in this act of reappropriation that we must pay attention to discourses of difference if we are to better understand what I call language ideologies of *in difference*.

Maybe we need a little less ethics and a little bit more encounter.

Gert Biesta

The notion of empowerment is quite prominent in education. I want to put forward another notion – the idea of education as disarmament because I think disarmament may have something to do with the whole question of how our souls can be touched. For me, the possibility to be touched has something to do with aesthetics and one concern I have is that a lot of education nowadays has become anaesthetic. It numbs our students so that they can quickly move through producing measurable learning outcomes and for me that's a travesty of education.

And although I think a lot of empowerment is done out of good intentions, there is a problem that before you know it, you end up in a mindset where the other is first of all seen as a potential threat; where the first interest for me is my own survival; and the future begins to be a kind of battlefield, where we all come empowered for the encounter. That's my worry when there is too much empowerment going on because you can say when you begin to empower, you begin to build a harness around yourself and that begins to raise the question, 'Can something still come through? Can you still be touched?'. And for me, this speaks to the danger that education actually becomes an anaesthetising process where students are empowered so much that nothing can enter any longer. Are these abstract concerns? Not for me.

So, how do we in cultural organisations create a space where people can meet as individuals?

Kate Fellows

We all put people in boxes in our heads either consciously or unconsciously, it's a natural human thing to do. This might be based on what they look like, what they say or indeed what they don't. Looking at or listening to me, you'll make assumptions about the communities to which I identify or belong. Through the information I've volunteered or what I'm wearing even, you may have decided based on that whether you think we'd get on if we went out for a coffee. And most of the time I'm okay with that.

The bit of the time I'm not okay with that comes from the negative side of the process. The bothering kind of 'othering' for me is recognising and often labelling somebody as different to you. It can have really positive effects of shared learning and empathy or it can have really negative ones of assumptions, misunderstandings and, at a very extreme level, hatred. The 'otherness' labels we give people often stay with them throughout their lives, and they may not be happy or comfortable with the assumptions and labels that others make.

So, how do we in cultural organisations create a space where people can meet as individuals? How do we create a comfortability factor where we can recognise the difference? I've tried not to assume things like the postcode of a school, which leads to another assumption of a certain attitude or a certain lived experience. I've learned to trust my instincts and try to be open about having difficult conversations, acknowledge my biases and my mistakes, be empathetic and curious, keep learning. All of these are now driven by what I see as my values of kindness, compassion and trying to be an empathetic human. I still ask questions of myself, I'm still learning.

The moment we start talking about languages in that way, there's a risk of losing the conversation that we want to have in the first place.

Angela Creese

Many of us here have been at the forefront of promoting a multilingual way of looking at the world rather than a monolingual way of looking at the world. But the moment you start talking about, for example, prioritising other languages at the start of a conversation with others, there's a possibility that if many others don't speak that language, then you don't join in the conversation. So, Jan Blommaert was always very keen to say, OK, that's great, let us all talk in a variety of different languages, but hey, you know that's not really the essence of the conversation because we may end up not understanding one another.

And there is a kind of argument in multilingual research that we should be first and foremost focused on demoting English in favour of other languages in particular contexts, so that somehow levels out the situation. But for me, the moment we start talking about languages in that way, then there's a risk perhaps of losing the conversation that we want to have in the first place. So I don't know. It's pretty controversial for me to say some of that actually, because I think I'm seen as someone who promotes multilingualism, but sometimes I think that discussion goes awry and we're talking about the wrong thing.

> **I was thinking about the notion of languages as possibilities or opportunities for doing and being different things.**

Tracey Costley

So, if we're moving backwards and forwards between different language practices or different named languages even, if we think about it in those ways – what do those kind of hierarchies represent in terms of established practices? Who gets to establish them? In what context were they established? And again, I'm just thinking through some of the things that we've been doing not only in terms of research methods, but also in terms of classroom practices around language teaching. In a sense, things happen in a certain way because we think that we've inherited certain systems and certain practices. And so changing our view of languages may enable us to change the hierarchies and with it the types of conversations that we can have, who can be part of them and how we join in and out of those conversations. So, thinking about languages in this way enables us to get at existing practices that perhaps maintain some of that inequality and present obstacles not only to access or to be able to manoeuvre, but also that restrict possibilities.

So, part of what I'm interested in is trying to disrupt some of those expectations. I want to explore how to do that and how to shift from a starting point that assumes a particular linguistic mode or where the assumptions are that you're going to be operating in a particular way.

I am interested in how to shift that and how to open up the discussion from the very beginning.

I think this is a period of change and it's really quite positive in the sense that there are lots of people working on this. There are lots of really exciting new publications about researching multilingually and how we do that. So, I think it is sort of there, it feels like there's a moment where things might be changing. But what parts of what structures need to be changed and how that happens remains, I think, an interesting question.

Irene Heidt

At some point in my work, I actually started using the notion of multilingual students instead of the official designation students 'with migration background' which is an ideologically loaded term that refers to individuals who were born outside of Germany (first generation) and those who were born in Germany to at least one foreign parent (second generation).[20] By multilingual I do not mean just speaking different languages – referring to a knowledge of separated linguistic systems – but having different ways of seeing the world, different ways of thinking and different ways of making meaning, even though we speak the same language.[21,22] So, those students in my provocation actually spoke German with the teachers, but they were drawing on entirely different discourses and different historicities, different collective memories, which ended up in those conflicting situations.

And I found it fascinating how Colin and you actually pointed out that our universities do not prepare us to do ethnographic work multilingually because the universities are so monolingually focused. And I agree with that and I found it's still paradoxical because that contradicts strategies of internationalisation in higher education, which also aim at international and (inter-)cultural exchange programmes, research and education – even though I recognise that these strategies of internalisation aim at instrumental and neoliberal goals. And so I was thinking, how do you define multilingualism? What would a multilingual ethnography look like?

Tracey Costley

So, Colin and I and other colleagues are involved in a large project looking at students or young learners in schools in Tanzania, Botswana and Zambia, and how their linguistic resources are or are not brought into classrooms. What happens in the community, what happens in the classrooms and the same for the teachers.

These students are existing in multilingual contexts. Yet, when they're in the classrooms, a very dominant model of language pedagogy and language instruction is happening. And our research looks at whether adopting a kind of translanguaging perspective – trying to have that sort of fluidity – is something that's possible in these schools.

In our first fieldwork trip to Zambia, we were thinking about how we do this during some of our meetings. Again, this is a largely multilingual group where there was a sort of default into English. And so we were curious about how we can interrupt that. So, in terms of researching multilingually, instead of leading with English as an opening for a meeting, perhaps getting another colleague to start in a different language so as to set the scene from the beginning that this was okay. And it was okay for it to feel uncomfortable. My own linguistic repertoire is relatively limited in this context, and that's fine. There are other things that I do and bring. And so when the meetings start, I can follow along and move in and move out. And so again I'm trying to make sure that we are doing things multilingually, collaboratively and responsively at all times with an awareness of how the language is working there.

Colin Reilly

I think this type of research has potential to be disruptive. Because if we think about it, me and Tracey are working in the UK. English is obviously the default academic language as it is for many countries around the world. I think our starting point is, as Tracey said, to view all the linguistic resources that we encounter – within the research, within the research team, as we're conducting the research – as valuable resources. In terms of education research, generally our team would have a position where we think pedagogically, the whole linguistic repertoires of students can be viewed as resources. So, we wanted to take that into our own research as well.

Researching multilingually is something that affects all stages of the research. This was important for us because sometimes there's an expectation of going out and doing your research and then maybe you need a translator at some point, and then that's when you start thinking about multilingualism. Something we were interested in was thinking about how it affects the planning and things like that and then how we engage with each other in our team. What languages do you need to use there? And then, importantly, thinking about outputs and things like that. How can we be disruptive within that and challenge this kind of English dominance?

Thandanani Gumede

When I reached the UK, I co-founded my own company called Zulu Tradition that began touring around the UK, and it also had a programme for schools. Education was a huge and integral part of everything that we were doing. So, for instance, if we did a showcase, we would perform for people, but we also had to deconstruct what we did and be able to explain and expand the significance of the music that we were doing in our culture.

For me, music and education are interchangeable. As a person of Zulu and Xhosa heritage, our history was not recorded but it was actually orally relayed and transmitted from the older to the younger generation, through music, poetry, etc. So, there is a lot in our music that ensures there is education, there is language and there is culture.

Thanda dressed in Zulu regalia (Thandanani Gumede)

I would go to different schools across the UK and perform with a group of other Zulus dressed in traditional Zulu regalia. We would only perform for 15–20 minutes. Afterwards, we would explain what we are wearing, including umqhele (a Zulu crown/headdress) worn by men, inkehli (a Zulu hat reserved for married women) and imbatha (the upper body covering). We would also speak about Africa in general: it is not just a place with trees, giraffes and lions loitering around, you know, they need to understand the contemporary aspect of that place.

We feel that education is part of everything that we do, because in Zulu culture, we have a thing called ukuthamundwa. That means information orally relayed, so we had to memorise songs to preserve the embedded knowledge. For example, my last name is Gumede. We don't have ancestry.com. We don't have things written down to say this is your ancestral tree. So, I have to memorise a sort of poem made up of my clan names (izithakazelo). Those are the names of my forefathers. So, if somebody else sings their poem and there happens to be a line that is similar to mine, then that would mean that we are related and cannot date or marry into that family.

So, this is why music, poetry and dance are important – they serve as the archives of our history. When they were teaching me to dance, I thought I was merely doing a dance but I later found out that they were teaching me to defend myself. So, those things, the subliminal education is ingrained in the music, the poetry, the drawings, the art. That is why when we go into schools, we insist that our music cannot be divorced from education. So we sing, we chorus and then we expound.

> The Indigenous presence in the exhibition space aimed to stop the general public just wandering through and looking at things. Instead it aimed to make them engage all of their senses to start to challenge unhelpful stereotypes.

Thea Pitman

My current research has focused on a 2018 arts-based project that aimed to create a positive space for intercultural exchange and the lessening of prejudice, on all sides, between Indigenous peoples and non-Indigenous society in Brazil.

On the first weekend of August 2018, a group of Indigenous people took over the Museum of Modern Art in Salvador, Brazil. The Arte Eletrônica Indígena project promoted the co-creation of electronic art between Indigenous and non-Indigenous artists and subsequently brought that co-created Indigenous electronic art to the Modern Art Museum for an exhibition. But more than an art exhibition, this turned into an occupation, a retomada of a space normally reserved for elite culture and its clientele.

Indigenous people starting to dance a toré at the inauguration of Arte Eletrônica Indígena (Dayanne Pereira, 2018)

Many prejudices circulate in Brazilian society about how 'Indigenous people can't use modern technology' and 'What are they doing with a mobile phone or a computer?' or 'What are they doing creating electronic art?'.

The interesting thing about the exhibition space was that it was in a site that attracted passers-by. So, it wasn't just preaching to the converted. And the Indigenous presence in town, in the wider urban space, for that opening weekend, was also part of this engagement with mainstream society. The Indigenous people went around wearing the project t-shirts which caused people to stop and ask questions. They used the space – through their presence and their performance of Indigeneity – to engage with this non-Indigenous audience.

The Indigenous presence in the exhibition space aimed to stop the general public just wandering through and looking at things. Instead, it aimed to make them engage all of their senses and to engage them in conversation about anything and everything to do with Indigeneity and art. To start to challenge unhelpful stereotypes that circulate in Brazilian mainstream society about Indigenous people.

> **Tawaná Kariri-Xocó:** When you mix electronics with our culture, with spiritual things, ancient things, crafts, it's about getting society to understand what it's like to be an 'Indian' these days. And I explain it all and people get the idea. People who would be afraid of talking to me and after they've stopped and talked, then they feel differently about things.

> **Mangatxai Camacan Ymboré:** It was a kind of cultural occupation because today we are recognised as being Indigenous more through our culture. If we don't show off our culture, we're not recognised as Indigenous. If I am dressed in my traditional clothes, showing off my Indigenous culture, many people will see that I'm Indigenous. They'll be curious and ask me questions.

> But if I'm daring to show my face here today, ready to fight, I've summoned the strength to speak up and tell people what it's like to be Indigenous. To say that I am Indigenous. I'm not afraid to say that that's what I am. I am Mangatxai and I came here to tell you that I am Indigenous and I'm going to fight for my rights.

> **Mayá Tupinambá Pataxó Hãhãhãe:** I even said to my colleagues, my brothers and sisters, my relatives in the community, I told them that we were getting ready to carry out a retomada at the museum, showing off our knowledge, our experience.

> **What happens in the encounter is that we experience a moment of being taught. We are being addressed by the world.**

Gert Biesta

This for me suggests, but I'm quite radical in some of my opinions, that the whole discourse about learning I think has little to do here. I would be happy to say, let's take learning out of education, because it's such an unhelpful notion. We should not think that we teach our students so that they learn about the other, because then they step into the game of explanation. I also don't particularly like the phrase 'learning from the other'. Because before you know it, you say, yeah, I use the other for my learning. And that's also not an encounter; it's an instrumentalisation.

Rather, what happens in the encounter is that we experience a moment of being taught; that we are addressed by what we encounter, by who we encounter; that we are being spoken to. And I want to claim the right, not just for other human beings to speak to us but I think that the whole world is speaking to us in all kinds of ways; that we are being touched, you could say. And there, I would suggest, we find the real educational question. The question we find in each encounter, namely – What is this that I encounter here asking of me?

And that's not a question that I can resolve by saying if I understand it and engage with it. Well, that's fine. That question – What is this asking of me? – is a question that interrupts, and therefore you can say it's an aesthetic question, because it potentially awakes you. And it wakes you in a very particular way, because the question – What is this asking of me? – puts me in question actually. And there, I'm no longer empowered. But I meet a moment of disarmament where you can say the encounter is precisely what pulls me into the world.

Teachers needed to be willing to be vulnerable and to be positioned as unknowing.

Rae Si'ilata

So, when we first piloted this work, getting teachers to work bilingually or multilingually with their Pasifika children was not normalised practice in English medium classrooms. So, we wanted to co-construct this with teachers so that they didn't get too defensive about it. Generally, teachers are used to holding power in classrooms, so we had to support teachers to actually have a choice and make decisions around how much they were able to put into practice.

And we noticed that when they felt they had ownership of it, they were willing to have a go. And so, what this meant was that teachers needed to be willing to be vulnerable and to be positioned as unknowing or as learners. Here's a quote from one of those teachers:

> I didn't know how to be culturally responsive. I remember that first workshop feeling out of my comfort zone and thinking how can I teach

using bilingual books when I can't speak Tongan, how can I teach in Tongan or Samoan? I remember that fear.

But she soon realised that just creating opportunities in her classroom for the children to become the teacher, she found that you don't need to be fluent in the language:

> You can let the children be the experts. They just step up and shine and it transforms your classroom culture. The children love it. It strengthens their literacy in English too because of the way you're working with the dual language books.

So, as teachers continued to engage in their professional learning and then to take risks around trying out these practices within their class-rooms: to move from monolingual to multilingual spaces or bilingual spaces and to be willing to make themselves vulnerable, they began to surface and recognise their own existing beliefs. This comes from one of those teachers:

> The bottom line is I failed this child and I have changed and I'm really emotional about this because if I failed him how many other children have I failed? And I've noticed that every single one of my children are now moving and this has all taken part in the last month or so it's hap-pened. Often we think we know it all; actually, we don't. I used to think I was a damn good teacher, and you woke me up on that day. I had to have a really good check of myself and my teaching practices and what was working and what wasn't and how I could change it and to this day it's affected me greatly.

So, as teachers became willing to share power, they started to learn from Pasifika children. Pasifika children were no longer othered in their class-rooms but, in fact, became the teachers both of other children and of the teacher. This teacher said:

> They're constantly translating for me but also they're talking to each other in their heritage language they love seeing me being the learner. They're at the point now where they will slow this speech down for me so I can repeat new words and they are the experts, and they are so proud. The change in classroom culture is mind-blowing. It's a culture of talk and expressing themselves; of being proud of who you are in your language and your country and accepting of everybody else's language and culture.

Thus, as they changed their practice and began to support children to make connections between their lived experiences and the schema in the book or the story of the book or the underpinning message in the book, the teachers actually realised that they had a real lack of knowledge about children's linguistic and cultural resources at home.

I can't read the books to them, but the book speaks to their worldview. These are their stories. Quite often our books do not intersect with children's worldviews like skiing holidays and feeding baby lambs on the farm. I hadn't thought about the stories that children bring with them to school. They all have stories that they bring.

Claiming Sameness, Claiming Difference

Not because we are like-minded but because we are different do we arrive to think differently together instead of merely confirming what we already know.

Charlotta Palmstierna Einarsson

Taking our community of ETHER speakers as an example, I realised that it's not merely that we come together here today but our coming together does something. It says something that it couldn't otherwise say. Gathering, even though we are online, enables us to think together in a way that we would not be able to do on our own or in another context. And meaning emerges from this thinking together. Not because we bring our various ideas just to create a pile of ideas but because we construct something new together that we could not have otherwise created – be that something knowledge or insights or new ways of looking at the issue of encountering the other. Not because we are like-minded but because we are different do we arrive to think differently together instead of merely confirming what we already know. The issue of self and other clearly compels inter- and multidisciplinary answers and I would like to comment that this situation makes it all the more important to recognise the diversity of the community gathering here today.

How does one achieve an individual positionality in regard to previously racialised or class or status or gender related speech forms and so overcome collective notions of linguistic authenticity?

Nigel Rapport

Your work, Quentin, is to try and end hierarchical, hegemonic and stereotypical determinations that are associated with speech forms and maintain a kind of collectivist apartheid in South Africa. If I was faced with that problem, my ethical proposition would be to do two different things. Firstly, an attempt to institute a neutral public language in the spirit of say Esperanto, a language that does not have any cultural, ethnic, collectivist history behind it; in which everyone is versed alike. Overcoming issues of differential cultural capital, overcoming issues of historical ownership, hierarchicalisation, etc.

So, on the one hand, one has a neutral public language. On the other hand, one guarantees private personal reserves, private spaces; where individuals express their selves to themselves and to significant others in individual ways. So, my solution would be a kind of bifurcation in usage. At one extreme, public and neutral; at the other extreme, private and idiosyncratic in which individuals' idiolects are given full rein, are allowed full expression.

How does one achieve an individual positionality in regard to previously racialised or class or status or gender-related speech forms and so overcome collective notions of linguistic authenticity? Because it seemed to me that Woman2Woman were going down this road in parodying collective speech forms and were doing it in a kind of individual way. I would want them to go further to explode notions of collective speech forms and say that as individual human beings, we each bring our personality to the collective forms of language. We inhabit them in individual ways, we personalise them, we animate them in individual ways. Rather than just parodying collective speech forms, explode the very notion that these things are linked to particular social groups. Public language is linked to everybody. Private language is linked to individuals alone.

> **I understand that we need to focus on the individual but that does not help us, many would argue, to work on the corrective, that is, the communities that need to be empowered.**

Quentin Williams

It's a very interesting question that you pose, and I think every language community in South Africa would disagree, especially the historically marginalised communities, because the current spirit of democracy is geared towards a future where the collective becomes empowered. The history of apartheid in Africa, especially among sociolinguists and linguists who need to atone for their linguistic sins because they were the most privileged, who went into coloured and black communities and documented the varieties as a collector, thereby also sustaining a misunderstanding of who that collective is by imposing a particular label on them. I understand that we need to focus on the individual, but that does not help us, many would argue, to work on the corrective, that is, the communities that need to be empowered. There are linguists who still insist that these varieties spoken by so-called coloured English speakers are coloured English. Language ideology of indifference has enormous implications for agency and the voice. Voice, that is, your ability to be heard, and agency, your ability to bring about institutional change.

I'm a great admirer of Esperanto and moving towards a collective understanding and moving out of the ethnic category that oftentimes multilingual speakers in our country are sort of locked into or boxed in. And currently, we are having a sort of violent public debate about origins of languages and different histories of formations.

So, I think the individual repertoire and understanding how that feeds into translanguaging or languaging have really shone a light on the multilinguality of South Africans and that sort of helps us to bust the myths and stereotypes of the speaker, different from what we came to understand in what I call apartheid linguistics. Because the obsession with apartheid linguists was Afrikaans and standard Afrikaans and that has meant that the other speakers – speakers like Woman2Woman – and the way that they parody creatively were pushed to the background. But now they are in the foreground and I think there is a focus on the collective more so than the individual.

Nigel Rapport

I just think that once you start essentialising membership of collectivities, there's no escape. It is a falsification of their individual humanity and their true individual identity by merely boxing them, labelling them, classifying them according to what I call fictional collectivities of class or status or profession or religiosity. These are cultural fictions that get in the way of the ontological realities of our humanity and our individuality, and once you start politicising them it's really hard to find a way to escape forcing people to identify by way of historical fictions that don't speak to their individualities.

> That is what was expected of me during Black History month – I had to be an organic echo chamber of pre-existing misconceptions.

Thandanani Gumede

In South Africa, I primarily focused on contemporary and American Gospel music, as well as jazz. And in the UK, I've been focusing exclusively, at least for my first decade here, on traditional warrior song and dance compilations. I am of Zulu and Xhosa heritage, and so the biggest struggle I faced when I was in South Africa regarding my performances: people expected me to sound American when I was in church. So, that was the default benchmark of my musical proficiency. My accent disappeared – it had to because the music was/is completely Americanised. And when I came back to the UK, there was this expectation that I had to sing in the click sounds. That is what was expected of me during Black

History month – I had to be an organic echo chamber of pre-existing misconceptions.

Fortuitously, about four or five years ago, Opera North created a particular project that I was so glad to be a part of because it allowed me to step away from doing what I was expected based on the way I looked and where I came from.

So, my work has shifted beyond 'what' I am to incorporate 'who' I am too, as an idiosyncratic individual – my work then became the conduit for that expression. Instead of just being put in an assigned box, I would reserve the elasticity to draw from any particular part of my life in order to express different things. All that I have been doing has been based on encounters. How do I resolve those tensions when, for instance, as a South African singer we were not allowed to sing with white people or people who looked diffcrent from us. How do I resolve those tensions so that they result in collaborations, in interactions?

> **How can somebody who has been othered by a majority culture, still encounter members of that dominant culture within their own shared language without being rejected, misunderstood, patronised?**

Helen Finch

How can somebody who has been othered by a majority culture, and who has experienced extreme violence at the hands of that culture, still encounter members of that dominant culture within their own shared language?

I'm speaking particularly in reference to my research[23] on the literature written by German Jewish survivors of the Shoah or the Holocaust, the mass murder of European Jews at the hands of the Nazis and other associated allies in the middle of the 20th century. This research encompasses a number of questions very germane to this project, particularly looking at life writing in the aftermath of trauma. The writers that I am looking at encountered violence at the hands of the Nazis because of being othered as Jewish, and yet they were people who shared a culture with their German persecutors, they shared a language with their persecutors. Often, they reflected on the fact that they knew their persecutors intimately as friends.

How can a German survivor, somebody who was born in the German lands, write in German to a German-speaking audience about their history of pain and suffering? How can they make a German audience – who in the 1950s and 1960s often wanted nothing more than to say that the past was over and done with; to say that enough compensation had been given to people who had suffered persecution; who wanted their literature to reflect an optimistic sense of moving forward from the past

– how could these writers find an audience? What role did their literature have in staging this encounter between Germans and Jews that would acknowledge on the one hand the shared culture, but on the other the radically different experience that German Jews had during the period of Nazi persecution?

Many questions emerge from this – the practical questions of what German publisher is going to publish this material that often accuses the German public of crimes and attitudes that it would rather forget? Such works might find a publishing house in other parts of the world. But when the people being accused of, for example, culturally persecuting Jews are the people who are publishing the literature – how does that encounter play itself out?

In fact, in many of the literary texts that I'm looking at, this encounter is fictionalised and restaged. Over and over again, the German survivor attempts to publish their work and yet it is rejected. Or in other fictionalised accounts, the German survivor attempts to testify in the German language to a fellow German only to find their witness ignored or in some way rejected, misunderstood, overheard, patronised or dismissed as being over-emotional, untimely.

> However, while such contextualisation can educate, it unfairly places the onus on the marginalised person to constantly explain themselves.

Parinita Shetty

For my PhD project, I created a fan podcast called *Marginally Fannish*. My guests and I loved different media, and we engaged with fandom communities in different ways. In our episodes, we explored how diverse groups of people are erased or misrepresented in media. We used the framework of our favourite fictional worlds, characters and events to discuss our real-world experiences and perspectives.

I was really lucky that a relatively diverse group of fans volunteered to participate. Together, we inhabited a wide range of identities – different nationalities, races, genders, sexualities and abilities. Since we were marginalised and privileged in different contexts, it wasn't really a case of me encountering the other because I was myself an other. Instead, different others came together in the podcast episodes and our conversations helped make up for my own gaps in knowledge about identities beyond my own.

Robert, one of my co-participants, discussed how in mainstream science fiction and fantasy media, magic or advanced technology is often used to fix and thereby erase disabilities. It's rarely used to imagine creative ways for disabled bodies and minds to navigate these worlds. He was deeply uncomfortable with the idea that his disabled mind and body don't belong even in most people's imaginary worlds. As he said, 'It comes back to the idea of always being told that a progressed world is a world which has eradicated you'.

Such conversations can act as consciousness-raisers and enable a collective process of decolonisation as people from both marginalised and dominant cultures become aware of issues they may not have previously considered. However, while such contextualisation can raise awareness and educate, it unfairly places the onus on the marginalised person to constantly explain themselves since the default in mainstream media and society rarely includes their experiences and perspectives.

For example, Robert found it difficult to explain what it's like to live with a disability because he's never experienced anything else. He's always had dyspraxia and he's always been on the autistic spectrum. He didn't know how his experiences differed from other people's lives.

Lara Stephanie Krause-Alzaidi

Helen, you mentioned the idea of the 'same other'. You also talk about language, some of what constitutes the sameness in your concept. How do you operationalise that concept? What is part of the sameness in the other and how you're using it?

Helen Finch

The question of sameness is about a cultural claim on the part of survivors, saying that 'the act of violence cast me out of the community'. During the Holocaust, obviously, there was an extreme example of excluding people and putting them into the 'zone of exception'[24] – dehumanising people, excluding them from the community of humanity, never mind the community of the nation. And the people that I'm writing about – H.G. Adler, Fred Wander, Edgar Hilsenrath and Ruth Klüger – make the claim: 'no, I have equal dignity and I have an equal claim to this culture'.

That's about equality, also saying this is my identity – you've tried to steal it, to take the language that I speak and to make it do violent acts, but I'm going to have a claim to that language. I'm going to have a claim to write literature in that language, in the way that I see fit. That might be drawing on traditions that are Jewish and have not been acceptable in this language; or it might be drawing on traditions that are traditionally seen as German and say, 'no, they belong to me as well'. So it's an act of reclamation – the sameness.

> One cares sufficiently about one's fellow human beings to ensure that they're given the space to come into their own and do not become mere means to others' classificatory ends.

Nigel Rapport

Society, culture, nationality, ethnicity, religion, class are symbolic fictions by which we classify the world according to insiders and outsiders, the same and different, good and bad, and by which we limit and fix, homogenise, stereotype and essentialise identities. But such symbolic constructs, literally fictions in that *we make them up and they remain dependent on our belief in them*, need have no place in the ideal vision of how human beings should be recognised and respected, including in a liberal society.

The problem of society, according to one of the founding figures of social science Georg Simmel, is that we only come to know the individual human beings with whom we interact by way of distortions, by the imposition of alien and alienating labels, categories and taxonomies.[25] We distort the other's individual identity when we claim to know them in collective and merely conventional terms as members of classes, nations, genders, religious communities, professions and so on. Simmel would describe this as the tragedy of social life. In response, I wanted to imagine a linguistic and behavioural style of public engagement that might be called 'cosmopolitan politesse'.[26]

In presuming the individuality of interacting citizens, cosmopolitan politesse does not expect an intimacy with them, doesn't claim to know or name another's private self. Cosmopolitan politesse is a medium through which to interact with anyone at a respectful distance. One cares sufficiently about one's fellow human beings to ensure that they're given the space to come into their own and do not become mere means to others' classificatory ends. But one does not wish or presume to know in any detail or seek to influence in any substantial way what another individual's coming into their own might entail.

Rosine Kelz

Emmanuel Levinas[27] criticises the Western philosophical tradition as a mode of thinking that aims to reduce the other to the same. He argues that it turns knowledge into a movement that domesticates everything it encounters, to make it fit into preconceived concepts, principles and theories. Similar critiques of modern epistemology are formulated by other 20th-century philosophers, as for example Henri Bergson[28] or Stanley Cavell.[29]

With Bergson, we can understand this mode of engaging with the world as seductive because it provides generalisable models that enable the successful manipulation of the material world. It makes the environment foreseeable and thus controllable. Cavell stresses that if one understands one's relationships to other people in terms of objective knowledge, this minimises the actual risks or challenges they pose to oneself. In that sense, framing the other as a problem of knowledge allows the self to deny its relational, vulnerable and finite character. For Cavell, human relationships would be better understood not in terms of knowledge but in terms of acknowledgement. Acknowledgement entails recognising that the other's pain requires a response. However, Cavell also points out that any response, any form of communication, always carries the risk of miscommunication and disappointment. And so, in this situation, even though Cavell assumes that we already share a form of life, a common language or certain assumptions and values, we still run up against the limits of commonality.

Maggie Kubanyiova

I think your talk illustrated how the moral connection is the starting point for tackling some of these big challenges. You have alluded to some of the tensions in our notions of sameness or universality and difference. I'm particularly reminded of Helen's point about sameness as a claim to a language, a culture, a claim to a shared space (see p. 46). And I wondered what your thoughts were on how we have been using the concepts of sameness and difference.

Rosine Kelz

Even when we want to talk about differences, the question of sameness comes back in. Many ideas of relationality require an understanding of an underlying sameness that is shared by all human beings. It is assumed that we need some form of common ground to be able to communicate. Some thinkers like Levinas or Judith Butler try to establish this shared ground by bringing in a bodily dimension. Sameness then, in a much more basic sense, can be understood as the shared experience of embodiment. I appreciate this argument to some extent. However, as Butler would also stress, we are not all embodied in the same way at all, and different bodies have very different sociopolitical standings. People do not all experience and see and feel their bodies in the same way. So, it's always this question of wanting to make a claim that we share something, but do we really need to make it so strongly?

Thandanani Gumede

There is one thing you mentioned, Ana, about initially focusing more on linguistics and grammar instead of the cultural aspects of language – and that sort of stayed with me. Something that can be an obstacle when it comes to certain encounters and in certain things being lost in translation. An example of that is someone who is Zulu coming to the UK, for instance. I remember coming to London, got on a train and I said hello to somebody on the train and they nearly called the police on me. And then I learned later that it is not appropriate to greet strangers in the UK.

But in Zulu hello doesn't necessarily mean hello, it means something else. Sawubona (singular) or Sanibona (plural) means 'I see you'. So, it means that I cannot start a conversation without greeting you first and, as such, starting a conversation without recognising that I see you is perceived as extremely disrespectful. And there is a premeditated dialogue to that greeting. I say Sawubona, or I say Sanibona if it's plural. So when you greet a person, there is this expectation that if you're younger you greet the person who is older than you as a sign of respect. So here in the UK, I was told that the grammatically correct response to 'How do you do?' is to repeat the exact same phrase back: 'How do you do?'. I was oblivious to the London cultural aspect, while my original greeting was intended to show respect for a stranger; it was perceived as the opposite and it ended in conflict.

I was wondering: after studying the linguistic aspect of it, does it become feasible then to completely understand someone whose culture you're unaware of? Because although you said language is music, which is a beautiful sentiment, I also believe that it is probably impossible to separate language from culture. Have you seen any difference since you started shifting your focus from that grammatical approach to looking at things from a cultural starting point?

Ana Deumert

Totally. I trained as a linguist, a historical linguist. I actually have a master's degree in what is called philology. I don't even know if that exists anymore. So, I was very much trained in a traditional disciplinary way. And for me, it was really when I realised that this isn't working. What I'm learning in the classroom and what I'm being taught doesn't resonate with my own experience of language, it doesn't resonate with how I live with language.

And I think art is important. I mean at some stage in my life, I wanted to be an actress and I was always very close to the arts. So, I was learning and thinking about language, as if language is apart from culture, as if language is apart from beauty, as if language is this system and structure. So I became a sociolinguist, perhaps now a critical sociolinguist. The more I engaged with my own feelings around language, the more my disciplinary orientation changed. Very much so.

For example, I'm actually not South African by birth, I'm South African by marriage. Xhosa, not Zulu, but yes. And it was interesting because yesterday when it was about introducing, I was wondering why I always introduce myself with my German name and never with my isiXhosa name. So, it's kind of an interesting question about introducing kinship, all of that, into the professional space. But when I grew up, I mean the language I spoke was the language of the streets. And it has little to do with German, that is the standard form of German. The cultural norms are so different. And hearing the language, the emotion the language can bring up, is different too. I didn't learn anything about this in the linguistics classroom. That a certain language, a certain way of speaking, can make me want to cry, that language can make me feel emotionally touched because it's so beautiful.

> I like this idea of solidarity and revolution, where political vision and dreaming, allow for connections that are not based on traditional ideas of sameness, but on a common purpose and respect for each other.

Lara Stephanie Krause-Alzaidi

My question to you, Helen, is related to the colonial and post-colonial history of contemporary Germany, which is where I think our work comes together. What I've seen in my research is that a lot of Black Germans are frustrated that it's always about the Holocaust, and it's always about that part of the German past. So, racialisation of others is silenced by this overwhelming genocidal history, which is not the only genocide that Germany has perpetrated. But the one against Black bodies is not really spoken about. Do you see any possibility of bringing together the force of these two debates or part of history, in order to effect change? And not always have this idea, 'This is overshadowing us and we have different issues', but maybe to think together and what literature could do in that context.

Helen Finch

I think the question is so interesting because this is exactly what the term 'memory theatre' is all about.[30] This idea of a public performance, with a predetermined outcome and a limited range of players who have a limited range of options that they can play. The idea of 'multi-directionality' comes from the American theorist Michael Rothberg where he talks about how the memory of suffering can be used to build community between excluded groups.[31]

So rather than the 'memory theatre' which sees excluded groups or minoritised groups somehow battling for attention in the public view, it's about building solidarity between those groups, seeing the commonalities and also the historical continuities between them.

For example, what happened in Germany, South Africa, and what happened later in Europe, and using those resonances to productively build solidarity that doesn't always have to be mediated via the white community.

Anna Douglas

The discourse of community has been a powerful sort of discursive framework for organising all sorts of practices. But actually, I'm really liking this shift that's been introduced by Rosine that is around solidarity with difference, that you can build solidarity and honour and recognise difference simultaneously, and I'm very interested in how that concept of solidarity, which, of course, in a British context is very much rooted in leftist ideology, which is why it's been replaced by community. It's emerged as a kind of anti-ideological positioning. But I'm wondering how we might begin to reposition the practices of solidarity with difference acknowledged.

Rosine Kelz

Definitely. And a practical question for me is what politics could look like if we do not start from a preconceived notion of community. I think this issue has come up a lot in social movements for migrant and asylum seeker rights in Europe, where the question arises how solidarity is conceived in situations where people are very differently situated in terms of resources and vulnerabilities and might not share the same political ideas on many points. In these settings, practices have developed that start off from taking care of basic needs and build community out of that, without assuming from the outset that we share the same broader political goals.

And then maybe from shared practices forms of political activism can build which revolve around a specific issue, but do not presuppose a pre-existing and shared social identity. I think both tactics of developing political interactions are important in different situations. Generally, it is worth re-examining ideas of solidarity, which in their histories already point towards the need to go beyond established forms of political community and political practice.

Ana Deumert

To me, the idea of solidarity resonates very strongly with my own thinking about positionality. I've always found the term 'ally' very problematic. It seems to me to be about the liberal subject, but it misses the deep collective commitment that shapes solidarity. The political scientist Jodi Dean[32] suggested that we should rather use the word 'comrade'. And I do like her suggestion. Jodi Dean notes that the word comrade indexes political and affective relations. She writes, 'no matter their differences, comrades stand together. They are united by a political vision, they dream of a different world, and actively struggle to achieve this world'.

A similar vision of solidarity was proposed by Kwame Nkrumah in the 1960s and linked discourses of revolution and African liberation. 'Comrade' first appeared as a term in the 16th century, when it referred to a person with whom one would share a house and food. Here, closeness was not, as implied by Derrida, grounded in the sense of emotional and affective sameness, but grounded in practices, in doing and in cohabitation. I like this idea of solidarity and revolution, where political vision and dreaming allow for connections that are not based on traditional ideas of sameness, but on a common purpose and respect for each other.

Linked to this is also the idea of love for others. We should not be shy to use this word – love – and to liberate it from its romantic connotations. James Baldwin's reflections provide inspiration. Love, for Baldwin, demands psychological and embodied self-transformation. We might not love everyone all the time, but we can engage with others, based on a practice that is informed by love.

Notes

(1) Zahavi, D. (2021) We in me or me in we? Collective intentionality and selfhood. *Journal of Social Ontology* 7 (1), 1–20. https://doi.org/10.1515/jso-2020-0076

(2) Crenshaw, K. (1989) Demarginalizing the intersection of race and sex: A black feminist critique of antidiscrimination doctrine, feminist theory and antiracist politics. *University of Chicago Legal Forum* 1989, 139.

(3) Ash, T.G. (2005) *Free World*. Gardners Books.

(4) Barad, K.M. (2007) *Meeting the Universe Halfway: Quantum Physics and the Entanglement of Matter and Meaning*. Duke University Press.

(5) Hau'ofa, E. (1993) Our sea of islands. In E. Waddell, V. Naidu and E. Hau'ofa (eds) *A New Oceania: Rediscovering Our Sea of Islands* (pp. 2–19). University of the South Pacific.

(6) Milne, A. (2017) *Colouring in the White Spaces: Reclaiming Cultural Identity in Whitestream Schools*. Peter Lang.

(7) Buber, M. (2002) *Between Man and Man*. Routledge.

(8) Gendlin, E. (2019) Interaction first, A PROCESS MODEL, land we belong to. See https://www.youtube.com/watch?v=xaopap6K_JQ.

(9) Gendlin, E. (2018) *A Process Model*. Foreword by Robert A. Parker. Northwestern University Press; Gendlin, E. (1997) How philosophy cannot appeal to experience. In D.M. Levin (ed.) *Language Beyond Postmodernism: Saying and Thinking in Gendlin's Philosophy* (pp. 3–41). Northwestern University Press.

(10) Schoeller, D. and Dunaetz, N. (2018) Thinking emergence as interaffecting: Approaching and contextualizing Eugene Gendlin's Process Model. *Continental Philosophy Review* 51, 123–140. https://doi.org/10.1007/s11007-018-9437-9

(11) Barad, K. (2007) *Meeting the Universe Halfway*. Duke University Press.

(12) Wittgenstein, L. (2009) *Philosophical Investigations*. (trans. G.E.M. Anscombe, P.M.S. Hacker and Joachim Schulte; rev. 4th edn by P.M.S. Hacker and Joachim Schulte). Wiley Blackwell.

(13) Carter, G.L. (2019) Ethical entanglements: Attunement and new materialist rhetoric. *WWU Graduate School Collection* 858. https://cedar.wwu.edu/wwuet/858

(14) Bennett, J. (2020) *Influx & Efflux: Writing up with Walt Whitman*. Duke University Press.

(15) Kearney, R. (1999) *Poetics of Modernity: Towards a Hermeneutic Imagination*. Humanity Books.

(16) Kubanyiova, M. (2008) Rethinking research ethics in contemporary applied linguistics: The tension between macroethical and microethical perspectives in situated research. *Modern Language Journal* 92 (4), 503–518.

(17) Heath, C., Hindmarsh, J. and Luff, P. (2010) *Video in Qualitative Research: Analysing Social Interaction in Everyday Life*. SAGE.

(18) Bion, W.R. (1967) Notes on memory and desire. In R. Lang (ed.) *Classics in Psychoanalytic Technique* (pp. 259–260). Jason Aronson, Inc.

(19) McDaniel, B. (2021) Popular music reaction videos: Reactivity, creator labor, and the performance of listening online. *New Media & Society* 23 (6), 1624–1641.

(20) Statistisches Bundesamt (2019) Persons with a migration background. See https://www.destatis.de/EN/FactsFigures/SocietyState/Population/MigrationIntegration/Methods/MigrationBackground.html (accessed 3 March 2019).

(21) Heidt, I. (forthcoming) *Conflicting Worldviews, Ethical Dilemmas, and Symbolic Power: An Ethnographic Study of Teaching Multilingual Students in the German Bildungssystem* (working title). Multilingual Matters.

(22) Heidt, I. (2023) When moral authority speaks: Empirical insights into issues of authenticity and identity in multilingual educational settings. In L. Will, W. Stadler and I. Eloff (eds) *Authenticity Across Languages and Cultures: Themes of Identity in Foreign Language Teaching and Learning* (pp. 165–180). Multilingual Matters.

(23) Helen would like to thank the AHRC for funding this research via grant AH/K002104/1 Literary testimony, transnational memories: The politics of transmission of Holocaust testimony in the German cultural field. It has been published as Finch, H. (2023) *German-Jewish Life Writing in the Aftermath of the Holocaust: Beyond Testimony*. Camden House.

(24) Agamben, G. (2005) *State of Exception*. University of Chicago Press.

(25) Simmel, G. (1908) *Soziologie*. Duncker & Humblot.

(26) Rapport, N. (2012) *Anyone, The Cosmopolitan Subject of Anthropology*. Berghahn.

(27) Levinas, E. (1991) *Totality and Infinity. An Essay on Exteriority*. Springer Dordrecht.

(28) Bergson, H. (2011) *Creative Evolution* (trans. A. Mitchell). Digireads.

(29) Cavell, S. (1999) *The Claim of Reason: Wittgenstein, Skepticism, Morality, and Tragedy*. Clarendon.

(30) Czollek, M. (2023) *Versöhnungstheater (Theatre of Reconciliation)*. Carl Hanser Verlag.

(31) Rothberg, M. (2009) *Multidirectional Memory: Remembering the Holocaust in the Age of Decolonization*. Stanford University Press.

(32) Dean, J. (2019) *Comrade: An Essay on Political Belonging*. Verso.

3 Encountering through Storytelling

Pinar, Glasgow
I miss my village. In my granny's garden she grows marigolds. I love the smell. I was thinking about how I dont smell that here in Glasgow so I bought some seeds and tried to grow marigolds here, on my balcony. They GREW! SO MANY! SO TALL! Now I can smell them every morning. The other thing I miss from Turkey is climbing up the cherry trees and eating the cherries.
Sophie Herxheimer 2022

Food stories collected live in ink – 1 (Sophie Herxheimer, 2021)

Whose Stories?

How do you leverage the power of storytelling to affirm and value others?

Dagmar Dyck

Students' artwork from Sylvia Park School, New Zealand, creating their 'How can we tell our story through visual art?' class project (Photo by Dagmar Dyck, 2021)

In our primary school, we do a whole-school inquiry every term. We always respond to a question and we integrate the arts throughout every inquiry. We've just done one last term and it was called 'how do we tell our story through visual arts?'. All the children had to produce an artwork, but it was an artwork with a story behind it. So, the story was just as important as the children's individual artwork. We have 520 students in our school, and 520 pieces of artwork were made in any medium that the teacher decided was relevant. But the most important was the emphasis around the child's story.

Ultimately, the stories that seem to matter to people are not perfect or trouble-free. They are filled with drama, failure, morality, symbolism, imperfect people, humble beginnings, loss, redemption, weakness and strength, consequences, courage, bravery and cowardice. Any quality that we can think of as part of the human experience or condition is in a story. Knowing this allows us full licence to be bold and courageous, to stand in our truth and let our stories be seen and heard. As an art teacher and as part of our school's localised curriculum, we understand the importance of equipping our students with the skills and confidence to tell their own stories. We do this powerfully through whole-school inquiries and through our integrated arts programme. I believe we do this so that

- our children can become more aware and strongly connected to the stories about places and people who have gone before them;
- our children might imagine or see themselves in those stories;
- that they build stronger identities through their knowledge and security with their connections and connectedness;
- they can begin to dream up and construct their own stories about who they are and where they are going to end up – we call this visualising;
- when they become leaders, professionals, mums and dads, teachers, knowledge holders, guides, storytellers, story writers and social actors in the future, they might feel a greater sense of connectedness and groundedness in who they are;
- that ultimately, the chances that those qualities will contribute to a greater awareness, acceptance and celebration of all our diverse and rich stories are greater if we become familiar with them when we are young.

From a teacher's perspective, storytelling can be conveyed through conversations and other means of communication, including the visual. Engaging in storytelling provides students with the opportunity to share unique experiences. It is an act of reciprocity, exchange and negotiation. The teacher's role is one of providing advice without confining the students' visions. The importance of supporting students' voices lies in making room for diversity and awareness.

What would my research look like if I had interviewed some of my students in some of the other languages that they use?

Tracey Costley

In my ethnographic work, I have always been interested in multilingual contexts. I've worked mostly in classrooms, trying to understand multilingual classrooms from the perspective of students and teachers and how classrooms come together in dealing with language and learning through other languages. But if I'm honest with myself and if I'm honest with the account of myself, I've done that research largely monolingually through the medium of English. Students or colleagues may have used or drawn upon other languages in interviews that we've done, but largely the context that I've been in has meant that even though the students or the teachers that I've been working with are multilingual, the process has been done, and very much so, monolingually.

My PhD was based in a primary school in London, and I was interested in English as an additional language learners. In the school, I think there were at the time over 50 or 60 different languages being used by members of the school. But given the kind of policy context of England, they were not necessarily being used as a resource in the classroom. My supervisors and the context where I did my PhD were very much attuned to language. But I'm not sure that I recall a conversation with colleagues at any point that asked 'what would my research look like if I had interviewed some of my students in some of the other languages that they use?'. And so it's interesting to look back at what I may have lost in my data potentially or what I may have gained, the trade-offs.

When I did interviews and focus groups, people were able to use whatever language practices they wanted. But when I asked why people used language in particular ways, the response was 'because, well, you're doing a PhD. This is academic research so we should be using English here because it's like a formal thing'. There was an expectation that people would have to tailor things so that I, the researcher, understood stuff, so that was what everything was accommodated around.

What does it mean for people to be valued? Does it mean they have to change who they are?

Rae Si'ilata

The Pasifika Early Literacy Project (PELP) has been operating in Tāmaki Makaurau/Auckland since 2014 with teachers of young Pacific learners or children. And, since 2020, we have also been working with teachers from English-medium and Pacific-medium early childhood centres.

So, this project really focuses on strengthening teacher capability to validate and utilise Pasifika children's languages, cultural resources and embodied experiences at home, at early learning centres and in schools. What we seek to do through the project is to normalise the utilisation of Pacific linguistic and cultural resources as essential foundations of Pacific second language acquisition, literacy learning and learner success. And it also supports Pacific children to see themselves, their ways of being and their funds of knowledge represented in the valued knowledges of schooling.

PELP uses the Ministry of Education's Pasifika or Pacific dual language books as windows into the lived experiences and worlds of Pacific children and as catalysts to support the utilisation of Pacific languages and our embodied literacies at home, at the centre and at school, focused on five Pacific languages: Cook Islands Maori, Niuean, Samoan, Tokelauan and Tongan.

Examples of Pacific/English dual language books used in early learning services and primary classrooms with the Pasifika Early Literacy Project (New Zealand Ministry of Education)

So, here's a couple of examples – getting ready for school both in Aotearoa New Zealand and in our island nations. It really supports families and children to see themselves and their valued funds of knowledge within the schema or underpinning or underlying messages of these books and to see their own embodied languages and literacies represented in the valued literacy of schooling.

The ETHER (Ethics and Aesthetics of Encountering the Other) question asks: How do people of conflicting worldviews, memories and future visions encounter each other? For us in English-medium education in Aotearoa New Zealand, it's crucial to provide dominant culture teachers with the opportunities to unpack their preconceived notions of the diversities of Pacific ways of knowing and being. In this sense, encountering the 'other' entails teachers seeing themselves as 'other'. When teachers see themselves through the eyes of children and families whose linguistic and cultural resources are different from those valued in educational settings, deficit assumptions surface and are disrupted, and transformational change begins to occur. In the PELP, we normalise bilingual and multilingual language and literacy practices, positioning monolingualism as 'other'. Through this approach, the linguistic resources and embodied cultural literacies of Pacific children, families and teachers are positioned as central to notions of success. Encountering the other in multilingual, multicultural contexts entails the teacher understanding how the child and the child's family might encounter the teacher as other.

We're working with teachers to help them to critically examine curriculum. Because the big issue is, we say to teachers, what does it mean for these Māori and Pacific children to be successful at school? Does it mean that they have to change who they are? Because within English-medium education, of course there are certain knowledge systems that are validated and valued traditionally. We're going through a big process here of decolonising and working towards transformational system change. But that takes time. So one of the big developments in the curriculum this year (2021) has been the development of the Aotearoa New Zealand Histories Project, which looks at pre- and post-colonial histories and saying that all of that needs to be taught in school. So that in itself will change the way teachers think about their own selves, and the way communities think about themselves within the context of schooling.

Nadra Assaf

For people who don't know, it's not always your typical thing to see 50+ year-old women on stage performing as a duet or solos. I was very harshly attacked by a critic in Lebanon who said that, 'Nadra Assaf would be better off performing her frantic menopausal issues in her own room instead of showing them to us onstage'. [laughs] So I was like, whoa that's really something!

Heather Harrington

We incorporated this text into a performance piece. I'm seated on a pool of red fabric with my legs open, moving the fabric, then neatly arranging it into a runway and finally removing it. And you know, just this imagery; blood, domesticity in the folding and straightening, preening on the red carpet… and Nadra decided to wear a costume that was very revealing, just a nude leotard. When this critic had seen her work, she was –

Nadra Assaf

Fully clothed, yeah.

Heather Harrington

We were supposed to perform this in Lebanon and we were going to invite the critic. [laughs] But then COVID happened.

Heather Harrington and Nadra Assaf on stage (© Kevin Colton)

Angela Creese

I've been very interested in the philosophical, theoretical conversation that Nigel and Quentin kind of started us off with (see Chapter 2) and the kind of pushback against some of that in terms of social categories and Nigel's argument about the importance of the individual here. And, of course, as a white academic at the end of her career, obviously I signify a particular thing to people before I even say anything. But what I loved in Heather and Nadra's piece was the reference to the menopausal woman.

I find myself really connected to many of Nigel's arguments actually, so it will be really interesting to pick some of these and the points he's making. But there are some categories that speak to you – and clearly that is about race and gender and all of the other big categories. I mean you so rarely see an older female body dancing. And I was really grateful you chose that kind of leotard, Nadra. It just means so much to me. It was one of those moments when social category and calling it 'the menopausal woman' was just so important. I just thought, wow you know that really is a voice unheard, it's a body unseen.

Amber Galloway-Gallego

In 2013, I was interpreting Kendrick Lamar's set, and someone recorded me and posted it – and the video went viral. It was seen by millions of people. This changed quite a bit for me. I was able to use my platform to start educating and advocating for our community on the importance of access to entertainment and to tell the world very loudly and clearly that we deserve access, and we should have access. But sadly, most of the comments in the comment section were always like 'How can deaf people enjoy music? Why do deaf people go to concerts? They can't hear'. So here's your answer.

> **Warren 'Wawa' Snipe:** So many deaf people love music. It's a big myth in the hearing world. They think that deaf people can't hear so therefore they don't like music, they don't like the sound. That is actually not true. Many deaf people love music. That's a fact. It's more about the feel and the way you vibe. We're just like anyone else.

> **Kristen Hejl-Rietz:** You ask me if a deaf person loves music. I would have to tell you I am one of those people. I am an absolute fanatic when it comes to country music like the incredible George Strait, Koe Wetzel, Cory Morrow, I mean the list goes on and on. I actually have a lot of music on my phone.

> **Sean Forbes:** Deaf people love music. For myself as a deaf person, I've always loved music. There have been several deaf people that have come up to me over the years and have told me 'thank you for making music accessible'. I've also met other deaf people in my life that music was not as important for them. But it wasn't until I got to the Rochester Institute of Technology that I met so many deaf people that love the music. And I've met so many more along the way.

So, I challenge you to flip the script when it comes to access. When places and events are set up, many of us are not even considered in the planning. Hearing people don't have to worry about whether or not you can hear your favourite artist because speakers are automatically provided but interpreters and captioning are often an afterthought or not even considered. Let's rewrite the story together. What if at events, at the planning stage, we made interpreters and closed captioning the same priority as speakers, microphones and lighting? Obtaining interpreter services and captions should not fall on the shoulders of our community, but it does. It sometimes takes days, weeks, months, even years.

Rewriting the narrative can be challenging but ensuring we are including all voices in the story will, in fact, promote a more equitable society. You are worthy of this, and I am too. We all are. We have the power to change the narrative, but this requires us to be open to the change which I know can be uncomfortable and that's okay.

Whose Tellings?

Adrian Blackledge

Erin, you said, almost as an aside, that you are not able to represent deaf people in Cambodia. And I think Jonathan had been somewhat apprehensive about representing the story, the narrative of a refugee. And I suppose it's an odd question but one that rears its head and has never been entirely solved, there's this question of who can represent who. Who gives voice to who, either in our research or perhaps in artistic practice as well?

Erin Moriarty

The ethics of the encounter, I think, is a very good frame for an examination of who the storytellers are and the responsibility of the storytellers. And one thing that I do want to say relates to how we inhabit roles that actually create otherness, such as in the role of an interpreter, not only between languages but also within these encounters themselves, such as in the case of British Sign Language (BSL) to English interpretation during conversations such as these. Sometimes, the interpreter becomes a barrier within the encounter as a direct connection is not necessarily happening. Multiple levels are involved here, not only with actual interpretation as a part of disability access but also in terms of our subsequent interpretations of these encounters, such as in presenting the narratives of the people we encounter, we are creating otherness and we need to acknowledge our complicity in creating difference.

Jonathan Dove

Thank you, Erin, for everything that you're saying there, but particularly the idea of becoming the other, I thought was a very helpful way of framing a lot of different activities. I thought that was certainly very helpful for me as a way of thinking about what I'm doing in trying to give voice to someone else's story and trying to embody someone else. I never thought of it in quite that way, but then I saw that it connects very directly with the act of signing, with the act of interpreting and with the act of translating. And there's a relationship between all of those. I found that very illuminating and thought-provoking, so thank you.

> Telling a universal narrative of the human species' inadvertent modification of the planet overlooks the fact that for many people the unthinkable catastrophe lies not only in the future, but also in their historical past or in their present.

Rosine Kelz

The discussion of the Anthropocene and climate change relates to the notion of encountering difference because much of the mainstream Anthropocene discourse still has an often-implicit tendency to talk about universal humanity and mean the experience of relatively rich people living in the Global North. People who, for example, could deal with a 2°C overall temperature rise, which would make much of the Global South uninhabitable. Glossing over the differences of how people are affected by environmental destruction and climate change today, I believe, is often linked to a wilful forgetting of European history of encountering those they have seen as 'other'.

Lewis and Maslin[12] propose the paradoxical date of 1610 as the beginning of the Anthropocene. This date is paradoxical because it marks not a spike but a fall in the CO_2 emissions in the atmosphere brought on by the collapse of the human population in the Americas in the wake of European colonisation. The unbelievable violence of European conquest, which brought epidemics, famine, war and slavery, led the population to drop from an estimated 54–62 million prior to the European arrival to about 6 million in 1650; so a 90% drop. Retelling the story of the Anthropocene as the history of European colonialism not only makes quite a bit of sense when we look at the CO_2 and methane emission records or the changes in fauna and flora, but it also highlights the political and ethical implications of picking specific Anthropocene storylines.

Seen from the perspectives of colonial history and post-colonial theory, European enlightenment and industrialisation are not a story of technological ingenuity and progress, spreading from Europe across the world – with the unfortunate but technologically fixable side effect of affecting planetary systems. Instead, violent colonial expansion was of key importance for setting in motion social and economic processes that enabled industrialisation in Europe. Colonial rule had lasting environmental effects around the world from the implementation of plantation agriculture, producing the cotton and sugar that fuelled early industrialisation in Europe, to the exchange of animals and plants, which has at least contributed to mass extinction events.

Moreover, European colonisers also violently imposed their understanding of human–nature relationships. These ideas, in turn, have played an important part in developing a capitalist mindset which sees the natural world primarily as a resource that can be manipulated and exploited for financial gain. Early modern thought, as well as political practice in settler colonies, has often linked the right to land ownership directly to its exploitation.

Telling a universal narrative of the human species' inadvertent modification of the planet which has now led us to the doorstep of a planetary environmental catastrophe overlooks crucial historical and contemporary differences between countries and socioeconomic groups. Those most responsible historically and currently for anthropogenic climate change are often the least affected by environmental disturbances. It overlooks that, for many people, the unthinkable catastrophe – that the world as they knew it is destroyed – lies not only in the future, but also in their historical past or in their present.

Thea Pitman

I'm interested in the ways that the Indigenous partners in the Arte Eletrônica Indígena project exercised curatorial agency during their time at the museum to effect a temporary decolonisation of the gallery space. Around 20 Indigenous people came to the opening weekend of the exhibition, and they really changed the way a standard hung exhibition works through their presence.

Ivann Karapotó taking a visitor's photo at the Arte Eletrônica Indígena exhibition (Thydêwá, 2018)

The picture is of Ivann Karapotó taking a photo of a non-Indigenous woman in the exhibition space who's got Indigenous body art beamed onto her body. If you have that kind of exhibit set up without the Indigenous people there interacting, that runs the risk of turning into an Indigenous kind of blackface where non-Indigenous people appropriate Indigenous aesthetics on their own bodies. But with the Indigenous people there, that changes the interaction in a helpful way, I think.

Travel writing, as a form, was exclusively for centuries a very white space. What we're seeing is an opening of this genre to a variety of authors who previously would not have had access to this heavily policed literary space.

Charles Forsdick

I'm going to suggest a rereading of a travelogue by Victor Segalen (1878–1919) titled *Équipée*, first published in 1929.[3] Unlike many other travel writers and colonial authors of the period, there's a tendency throughout Segalen's work to acknowledge the travelling or mobile nature of other cultures. So, the Polynesian or Chinese protagonists of some of his most important works are themselves travellers. And this understanding of the travelling nature of other cultures and of the potential of their inhabitants to be travellers in their own right is radically different from that of the majority of his contemporaries.

These ideas are translated via the travelogue *Équipée* into a reflection on the traveller–narrator's relationship to and his representation of the 'travelees' he meets. For instance, a Chinese girl who stares at the French traveller produces a troubling moment of contact as the narrator is himself exoticised and, according to Mary Louise Pratt's logic, studied from the perspective of those who participate on the receiving end of travel.

All of the works sketch out what Victor Segalen calls an aesthetics of diversity. They were written during a period when colonial literature and the exoticist novel were at their height. They attempt, though, to produce a narrative perspective that either recreates non-Western voices or is at least inflected or attenuated by the multiple perspectives that constitute any form of inter-human and intercultural encounter. The aim of this provocation is to explore the ambiguities of Segalen's engagement with the ethics of travel and, by extension, to reflect on the ways in which travel narratives can present contact zones as spaces that highlight the initial discomforts that encounters with difference are likely to produce.

What was original in Segalen's work – produced in a context characterised by the still often unquestioned assumptions of colonial expansion – was its reflection on the relationship between Western self and non-Western other. In the field of travel, to borrow the terminology of Mary Louise Pratt[4] in the context of her thinking on the contact zone, this translates into a reflection on the connection between traveller and 'travelee'.

Segalen's own travelogues pose clear questions about the ethics of travel and, in particular, about the asymmetries of power that such meetings often imply. He presents these encounters in terms of a mutually disorientating destabilisation of identity. This is dependent on an understanding of exoticism that is profoundly bilateral and depends ultimately on an imagination of mutual defamiliarisation. According to this, the traditional solipsism of the European traveller is undermined. And this goes on to challenge a critical orthodoxy in the Anglophone academy where the founding and enduring influence of critics such as Edward Said and Mary Louise Pratt has often meant that travel literature has been read as a form of colonial discourse.

This is travel writing that's emerging very much in a colonial context. And so, those issues about the subject of travel – what Mary Louise Pratt calls, I think really usefully, 'the travelee' – literally the person who is travelled over and who is often marginalised and domesticated in the account.

For me, it's the key question about the form. It's a form which, as I implied, was for centuries an exclusively very white space. And so what we're seeing is an opening of this genre to a variety of authors who previously would not have had access to this heavily policed literary space. The other thing that really strikes me is an understanding that travel writing has for many years created a very elite understanding of the practice. And that we need to be open to multiple journeys, many journeys that are enforced, that are necessary and that relativise the types of journey that I talked about very briefly in my provocation – challenging the journeys of Victor Segalen in China, who is there not only as an archaeologist, a French colonial official and military officer, but is also engaging with a series of questions that he intuitively anticipates.

So, I think in the 21st century, I go back to really what was at the heart of my provocation, this sense that travel writing, despite all the historical baggage it freights, remains a form in which we can grapple with a number of the issues that bring us together today from our multiple sectors and perspectives, and with our interests in a diverse range of media.

What are you asking when you're asking somebody to tell a story?

Louise Dearden

Last week, during the half-term break, I had interviews with students who had agreed to participate in my PhD project. As a prompt for discussion, they had all created collages with images that symbolised important areas of their life. Henry's collage contained nothing of the sort. When I questioned him about it, he made it clear that he does not like talking about himself in class. He had covered his paper with images from the newspaper story about the Vietnamese migrants who had perished in a refrigerated lorry. Two weeks earlier, when this news story had infiltrated our class, Henry had not joined in the discussion; in fact, he moved himself to another table and turned his back on the conversation. Yet, on the same day, he waited until his classmates had left and then chose to share his experience of travelling to the UK. His journey was a traumatic one. He came by boat... but he can't swim. He knows of people who came in lorries... and not everyone made it. In his interview, he continued drip-feeding more pieces of his story. They were fragments, but I still felt privileged.

Today is the first day back after half term and at the end of class, I'm collecting the reading logs. Henry doesn't have his on the desk so I don't ask him for it. He hovers waiting for the others to leave. I resist the temptation to grill him over his lack of participation and instead I ask him what story he will tell for his project. He squirms on the spot, looking very uncomfortable with the question. He frowns at me and says he doesn't like stories. He doesn't elaborate. I presume this is why he hasn't bothered with the reading log. So, imagine my surprise when he pulls from his bag a completed reading log. He is desperate to show me, and he is animated as he talks me through some computer-related user guides he's read. When he's finished, for the second time in our short relationship, he makes it clear that he does not want to talk openly about his reading and his goals in front of the other class members. And he doesn't want to tell his story.

Henry's portrait collage; this was to be used as an interview guide (Photo by Louise Dearden)

Jonathan Dove

A new piece of music often begins with an encounter: someone has a dream, a hope, a wish, they want a composer to bring something new into the world, and the composer has to listen and imagine what they might be trying to hear. A few years ago, I was asked to write a lament for the refugees who have died crossing the Mediterranean. I suggested that, instead, I tell the story of just one refugee who survived the Mediterranean crossing.

A choir in Bristol joined forces with a performance venue to commission the work, and we agreed we would like to talk to refugees in Bristol. I had already read Gulwali Passarlay's *The Lightless Sky*, his first-hand account of his journey from Afghanistan to England. He set out when he was 12. The journey took him a year.

Because he had told his story so vividly, and because I had also read other refugees' accounts captured in such books as Patrick Kingsley's *The New Odyssey*, I naïvely imagined that it would be easy to meet refugees in Bristol who would be prepared to talk about their experiences to me and to my collaborator, writer Alasdair Middleton.

Some years earlier, Alasdair had been involved in another project exploring journeys to the UK. He had written the libretto for an opera based on interviews with the parents of pupils at a London school. All those parents had a story to tell about how they had come from abroad to live in London. The hard thing was to choose from so many stories. We imagined our Bristol task might be similar.

And this reveals the inadequacy of our imagination and experience in this particular situation. Even though, as we read a refugee's story, we were making the journey ourselves in our minds, we had completely failed to grasp how traumatic it was, how overwhelmingly painful the many kinds of abuse and suffering involved along the way, including encounters with the British authorities. When we put out word that we would like volunteers to tell us their story, we did not realise what we were asking. We had not imagined the level of care that would be needed to support a refugee reliving recent experiences.

So, we were puzzled when Bristol refugee organisations agreed to help us, but this somehow never seemed to lead to meetings. We realised that issues of trust might be involved, and there was also no particular reason why refugees would be especially interested in the kind of piece we were thinking of making (a stageable oratorio, you might call it). But we were a long way from understanding the situation.

Louise Dearden

The storytelling operates on several levels in my provocation. First of all, it was the medium that I chose in order to communicate what *I* was feeling. Because this has ended up very much as my lived experience

– from trying to get to understand my students initially on what I could do for them to give them more than identity labels to draw on like refugee or English for speakers of other languages (ESOL) student. It has come full circle and now I wanted to show with my storytelling how I was affected by the whole process. So, the genre of a novel was an ideal medium for me. It also makes it easier for audiences who are not necessarily academic to access. So, on that level, I found it a way of showing my analysis, without telling, without summarising – but instead showing it like a dramatic scene. I'm pulling in the reader. I hope that's what it will end up doing – pulling the reader in and giving them a chance to experience what I felt.

And, like Jonathan said earlier, my shortcomings. It's made me quite vulnerable, I think, in places. You can see it in the story – the way that the students are given the space and I allow them to tell their own stories, so on another level, when they want to tell them. And also the way that they kind of subvert the norms and expectations of our space. It's not considered 'normal' in this kind of space to allow the students to dictate what happens, but very often the stories take over. So, on that level, Jasmine tells her own story, Henry refuses to tell his story until he's ready to tell his story.

And again, this goes back to what the others were saying as well about the idea of, 'what are you asking when you're asking somebody to tell a story that you know is possibly an upsetting one?'. The task that all the students were set was probably very well-meaning to give them a chance to come and join in a competition – their stories would be published on the website. But although they enjoyed the stories that we were telling between ourselves less formally, the idea that their story would be put onto a website was almost horrifying for some of them. And I wonder about how ethical some of our ESOL activities really are when we're trying to tap in and get personal information out of students that is very traumatic.

Sophie Herxheimer

My provocation is about my long-term project that I've been doing since about 2004 and it's got a rather unwieldy name. It's called 'Collecting Stories Live in Ink'. It's a way that I work which involves temporary collaborations where often I've been asked by an organisation or a residency or a project to work with members of the public or a community group in collecting stories mainly because these people who ask me to do it have seen me do this before. And they realise that this is a nice way to involve people in art, in thinking and sharing and listening and stories. And, I don't know, it's a kind of immediate thing because as an artist and a poet, I've often worked using instinct and spontaneity and interaction.

It's a genuine exchange because each person gets a copy of their story to take away. They are my collaborator, they are 50% of the art. What they tell me goes in the art, they're the material, the content. I'm the drawer and the servant of the story. So, it's a very funny arrangement but somehow it suits me because I'm a poet and an artist, and using words and pictures together is my natural state of being. So, I like the fact that I can use both and that I can dovetail the image with the text and the listening with the looking. It feels like what I should be doing and so luckily for me I get plenty of opportunities to do it.

a traditional Zoroastrian dish is called 'bheja noo cutlet' It's goats brain with chutney, breaded and then fried. I dont eat it. I'm a vegetarian! Shireen, South Kensington

Food stories collected live in ink – 2 (Sophie Herxheimer, 2021)

And then we developed this project further, which was partly provoked again by Clare Patey, because she invited me to make a tablecloth big enough for a thousand Londoners to dine on together. On hotel-salvaged linen, I made a 300-metre tablecloth. I screen-printed it at London Print Works Trust and in each place setting, I put a food story that I'd collected from a Londoner. At that stage, I wasn't always collecting them live, especially as I had a deadline. So, I would collect them from people at bus stops, in the shops – anywhere. The school playground when I was picking up my kids: 'tell me, what do you like to eat? Who did the cooking in your house when you were growing up? Mhmm that sounds nice!'. So, you know, I always had my notebook and my pen.

When we had Feast On The Bridge from 2007 onwards, I guess my tablecloth started its life and probably ended in 2012 because then the funding was cut for Feast On The Bridge and the Thames Festival in general. But every year, I would have a stall on the bridge, and I would collect people's food stories live in ink. And I'd have a big wad of paper and a photocopier and a helper who's known as the photocopier whisperer because an outdoor photocopier always goes wrong – or even indoors they do, don't they? – and a big bottle of ink, a nice set of brushes. And I would just sit there and listen, and one by one people would tell me their stories. And I would draw the stories for them and I would also write as close as I possibly could in their own words. In doing that, I had to really tune into them and find out what was important in the story. Because if somebody talks to me for five minutes – you can imagine that's like a storm of thousands of words. So where do you start? What do you choose? What line do you begin with, what line do you end with?

The theme of food, which is a great theme, is obviously a universal theme because hopefully everybody gets to eat quite often. And it connects to our families and our stories and where we come from and who we are and where we're going and what we like and what we don't like and our senses and all our relationships, our belief systems – they're all tied up with food. So, food is a great universal theme to go in at.

Performance and drama can be a really useful tool to display research and to make it more accessible.

Mohasin Ahmed

The first thoughts I had from yesterday when thinking about the other and how we encounter the other were some of the discussions about language. The first thing that came to mind was that some of the language that has been used over the past two days might not be as accessible to people who are not from an arts and humanities background, or an academic background. I think that's an important point when we try to think about how we can include the other, because obviously a lot of people from groups that may be marginalised, or may experience more inequalities, may not have a chance to engage with opportunities like this. So, I think that opening things up and thinking about language, not just in terms of cultural languages or sign language and different forms like that, but also in terms of fields and if it's just very specific to a field or if it's easy to read for a lay person.

One of the prompts that was shown asked, 'Is performance or drama a good way to display research?'. And I think that ties into what I've been thinking because movement and dance and the body is something that we can all understand because we all have a body. And seeing that experience being played out is something that can be quite beneficial to people who might not be able to understand the words or the context of things that are being discussed. So, I do think that performance and drama can be a really useful tool to display research and to make it more accessible.

> We have an ethical responsibility to represent research for academic and general audiences to affect them. To *affect* them!

Joseph Valente

I feel that we have an ethical responsibility to 're-present' research in ways that push back against the traditional boring research that disconnects us, that disaffects us. However, we also get promoted because of our research. But who does this benefit? What good does this actually do? If no one reads your research, it is like the riddle of a tree – if it falls in a forest and no one hears it or sees it, did the tree really fall?

In the context of our work with kids with disabilities and deaf kids, there are real consequences for our work not being read or seen or taken up by people. I get that we have no control over how it is taken up. I get that. But I also feel like we have an ethical responsibility to represent research for academic and general audiences to affect them. To *affect* them! To inspire them, to inform them, to PISS THEM OFF! about the things that are happening to those less privileged than us. To me, it's the ethics of aesthetics. If we write or represent in sterile ways, we cannot be surprised by the fact that folks take up our work in sterile ways or don't even pay attention to us at all.

Ana Deumert

You know, at the moment, I am trying to better understand language and signification. My engagement with music and music theory, specifically jazz theory, has really opened up a space of saying: language is music. And everything else we have said about language is incomplete and we have closed ourselves off from what is actually most amazing about language. And that is its musical quality. Because we have emphasised the syntax, the structures and all of that. And I think once we do that shift, it opens up everything. I mean, poetry has been kind of taken out of the linguistic realm because you can break the rules of language. But that's what it's all about. That it has that quality, that it invites us to think about language, and meaning, beyond it being a rule-governed structure.

I've always wished to have a teaching space in which we could dance language, to come back to ballet and performance. Can you dance your language? What are the shapes, the bodily shapes that you associate with your language? At the University of Cape Town, we also work on topics of language endangerment. This includes the lost languages of the Western Cape. And it is the whole embodiment of the language and the revitalisation effort that attempts to bring languages back into the public sphere that are so closely linked to art. It is not about writing grammars and dictionaries. It's about art. It's about feeling the lost language in your body, singing it, dancing it, experiencing the music. So, I think also that the way sociolinguists have phrased revitalisation efforts as in 'we've got to document and write a grammar and the dictionary' often does not reflect the way speakers experience it as a very lived experiential and artful experience. That is what matters.

> When people collaborate, when people do encounter the other, there's always a third thing made, which is the connection. And it is that third thing that is made that is the magic really.

Sophie Herxheimer

I suppose when people collaborate, when people do encounter the other, there's always a third thing made which is the connection. And so a collaboration forces a third thing in the room which has its own personality and that is the collaboration. And it is that third thing that is made that is the magic really. Because it's this sort of uninvited extra which is partly to do with spirit. And because we live in a very secular age, it's very hard to use the right words to pin it down. And that's why I was quite interested in Cornelia's presentation (see pp. 105–107) where the magic was actually God and religion in the church collaboration between the African church and the German church there. And I think in secular situations, it's harder to know where you're going to pin down that ephemeral quality that is spirit and connection actually. And it's to do with the souls of the people involved meeting on another plane that isn't literal and isn't about what everyone had for breakfast.

It is ephemeral in something like music. It stays in the air and when the music's over, it's not in the air anymore but it's sort of gone into everybody. And so I met with a poet who I had to draw for a commission once; a wonderful poet who I truly admire. And she'd written an amazing book which I can't even remember the title of. [laughs] And I said something like, 'Oh there's something about this that's magic'. And she said, 'Yeah magic. It's the only thing left to believe in'. And I was struck by that. And I use the word casually but I don't think it's really casual.

Ana Deumert

I like what you're raising by bringing in these three words – moral, love, magic! This is something that we are trying to reclaim in the social sciences, a conceptual space that has traditionally emphasised its association with the sciences and said: 'we are sciences, we can do correlations, we can do statistics and so forth'. Thus, all of that which was always part of art has just been pushed aside. And that's why it seems so challenging as a sociolinguist trained in what is ultimately a structuralist discipline, in terms of training and its history, to start thinking about something like love. And you mention it at a conference, and you think everybody will just look at you like 'what's going on now?'.

Magic – I mean when it was brought up, I was thinking of Sylvia Wynter's work on humanism as enchantment[5] – the re-enchantment of the world, the need to re-enchant the world. For me, that's what magic is – this enchantment of the world. We've kind of let it go and now we have new philosophical traditions that are bringing in love – actually they're not that new but they're being rediscovered. And morals and magic and the re-enchantment of the world and spirit, spirituality.

I find this very interesting because I currently supervise a postgraduate student who is working on spirituality, and I realised that we actually don't even have the vocabulary in sociolinguistics. We really struggle with it. We need to find these words. And that's why the turn to art is so helpful because suddenly the words are there. Maybe not as 'academic' concepts, but as a felt experience. A musical piece can explain what I'm not managing to capture about something such as spirituality.

Adrian Blackledge

I absolutely agree with you that we should be making the most of the arts in representing the social research data that we collect in our observations of the social world. We should be setting the data to music, we should be creating theatre, we should be creating dance. And it's something we've started to explore and I'll just give one quick example.

Some of the sociolinguistic research that we've been doing was an observation of a volleyball club. The team included players from 11 different countries, and the coach was from Hong Kong. One of the first things we noticed as we observed them practicing was that there was something balletic about their practice routines. They seemed to us to be dancing. It was so rhythmic; they seemed to be dancing their practice routines. And so, when we came to write this material up, we didn't just write research reports and monographs, but we also went to ethnographic drama which gave us the opportunity to represent the volleyball practice as ballet or as a chorus line on Broadway. So, the actors become volleyball players, but then the volleyball players become dancers in a chorus line or in a ballet.

Without taking an artistic approach to the representation of that material, all we could say is, 'it seemed to us to be reminiscent of ballet'.

That's so weak and lacks all power. It doesn't resemble at all the experience that we had. But actually to put it on stage, to have people doing that dance and coming in and out of role and becoming dancers on stage seem to us to have the potential to be far more powerful. So, I just want to agree with you that we need to make the most of the arts in representing and, I suppose, almost going beyond the observed material.

Angela Creese

Yeah, and I think it's also about the polyphony of different voices and the fact that there's a duality there. Those voices contradict one another, they're ambiguous, they're not kind of always straight. Because in academic writing, typically the line of argument gets carried through very heavily in a journal, and you're not able, even in ethnographic writing in an article format, to often hold on to the contradiction and the ambiguity of different voices. So yeah, that polyphony, I think, is important.

> Our job is constantly to make a case for the world, and say to the student, 'look there, turn your attention to the world'. What the world may be asking of the student, that's not our business as teachers

Gert Biesta

I once shared my critique of culture with a colleague who was a professor of anthropology and she said, but if we give up on culture, then our whole field ceases to exist. I think it's important that ethnography resists explanation, because that gets you into a very problematic relationship, and quite similar to how I try to resist explaining my students to myself or to them. But from what you say, there are other sort of modalities of ethnography – you call them representations and I think what they do is they become educational. Because what they do is to try to frame attention in a particular way. So, to say we write an ethnographic play is not just a way to represent, but it's also actually a way to present so that it can focus attention for the ones who watch the play.

And for me that precisely turns the question then to the ones who watch the play, for example, or read the script, because then it becomes a question for them, what they do in that encounter. And that's completely the opposite from saying 'we as ethnographers can provide the explanations, so that everyone can have happy intercultural encounters'. Because then you end up in an impossible position. So, I think where you're going not only makes it educational but it also turns the question where I think it should be. Not in how you can explain, but in how you can focus attention so that it opens up a possibility for people to say, 'okay, so there is something here for me to figure out'.

Another book that has really inspired me, or actually a whole body of work, is from the German educational scholar Klaus Prange who says that zeigen, which means both to point and to show, is fundamental to education. It's because it does two things at the same time. The teacher points and says to the student: 'look there' or 'listen to that' or 'pay attention'. But in one and the same gesture, the teacher also points to the student and says, '*you* pay attention'. And there you can see something of the triadic structure of teaching. The teacher, the student and something – I would call it the world, Prange calls it the theme, you can say the issue. Now you can say that the work of education is how you can realise an articulation between these three elements.

Teaching tries to focus attention, but we can never enforce our students' attention; we can never control the attentiveness of our students. So, we may manage to direct or redirect the attention of our students, but what they do there, that's up to them. And we can stand there with expectations and hopes, but not with control.

And I think this is partly the beauty of the point here that you can say, if education is fundamentally about pointing, in that form you can already see that the freedom of the student matters. That's, of course, not this neoliberal idea that to be free means to do what you want to do – what I call the freedom of shopping, where you just walk into a shop, grab what you want and walk out without any consequences. Rather, it is the freedom to attend to the world and in meeting the world, to encounter yourself in relation to the world. And for me this highlights that in the pointing of education the encounter is central.

That has something to do with the aesthetics of education, the idea that education somewhere has something to do with the touching of the soul. But here, I want to at least remind myself that it's not the teacher who is the toucher of the soul of the student. Before you know it, you end up entering moralising education where the teacher says, 'I'm going to touch your soul in a particular way'. We are in a very different position – this is this strange second-person position. Our job is constantly to make a case for the world, and say to the student, 'look there, turn your attention to the world'.

What the world may be asking of the student, that's not our business as teachers. You can say that in that encounter the 'I' of the student is called into existence in a very different way from the modern 'I' that stands in a perspective and views the world.

I always do what is best for the musical resonance.

Maya Youssef

Fast forward to now, to my provocation from my latest album *Finding Home*. I have been performing everywhere and I have been expanding my musical expression with different tools. *Finding Home* is about the state of feeling at home, as opposed to it being a place. And one of the pieces that was composed as part of the *Finding Home* album was commissioned by Opera North. And it was recorded by a stunning quartet from Opera North's orchestra.

When it comes to putting a musical instrument that is so traditional such as the qanun with a string quartet which comes from the Western music tradition, a lot of people ask me, 'are you trying to create a West meets East experience?'. And my answer to this is that I always do what is best for the musical resonance, for the emotional resonance of the piece as opposed to having a logical reason for having a string quartet. So, for this piece, for this lullaby, I wanted the deep voices and sounds of the quartet to be a sonic representation of the mother's hug.

So, a bit of background about this composition is that I have seen an image of a mother fleeing for her life, holding her baby, singing for her baby – with a bomb blast in the background. And she is moving forward towards this better future for herself and her baby, singing, ignoring the sound of the bombs. And for that I wrote *Lullaby: A Promise Of A Rainbow*. Because we all hold on to this promise. And the quartet was really to bring in the voice of that mother who can be from anywhere, from any conflict zone, not only from Syria. And she is taking herself and her baby to that land of hope, to that land of the rainbow.

I started writing music because of the war in Syria. I was not a composer, I did not have any need to write. And there was a moment when I saw an image of a small girl – who was the same age as my son – dying in her bedroom, that I held my instrument and music started coming out from me while I was in tears. So, I was forced to do it, really. So I can heal and I can make sense of what's happening in the world. And from that point onwards, the music has become my tool to really translate everything, all of this income that is coming from all over the world – the war, the trauma, seeing my friends dying, seeing places I love destroyed. I started to see myself as a human filter – and going back to Awad mentioning that music is joy – you know it is joy for me always, but also it's a way to encounter these dark corners of the heart. Where you are in a state of absolute despair and darkness, and just giving light to these spaces and hopefully in doing so, giving them an opportunity to heal in some way or other. And in doing so, for me, writing music is part of my spiritual practice.

Whose Listening?

Anna Douglas

I've just worked on a project – which I didn't realise was going to have this outcome at all – where I worked with three Chinese students who wanted to work with a group of migrants. They come from Politics MA and they wanted to work so I set them up in a context that was the art gallery at the university. And we talked about a way of working with the migrants that was tied to a project that was about slow looking – where you really take a long time to look at a painting and you use it as the prompt, to elicit storytelling and empathy. What was so interesting was that I encouraged those three students to think of themselves as migrants. Because actually they've come to this country from another country and although they've come to study, a definition of them could also be that they're migrants. Now, they'd never thought about that before, that they themselves could be migrants. And in that exchange with other migrants, what was so interesting was that the other migrants commented in their feedback, how interesting it was for them to have a project led by other migrants.

Witnessing allows us to experience 'the manyness of worlds'.

Ana Deumert

I've recently become interested in María Lugones's idea of witnessing.[6] It is a useful concept. It is not just listening or seeing, an approach that privileges the ears and the eyes. But as we are in each other's presence, we are fully and bodily co-present, feeling with all our senses, witnessing the other, the fullness of their being, their joy and pain, their hopes and anger. Witnessing allows us to experience what Lugones calls 'the manyness of worlds' and to lead a life that is plurisensical, not monosensical. A plurisensical life is, I would suggest, a life that is magical, artful, attuned to multiplicity and mutuality. It is art, in particular, that attunes us to the manyness of worlds, that permeates our boundaries and makes them porous, open to receive.

Thandanani Gumede

So, with the People's Lullabies project, we had to work with different organisations that are Opera North's partner groups. Organisations such as Caring For Life that supported people with learning disabilities and there were groups that worked with ex-offenders – women ex-offenders – and even old people's homes. In encountering these different people it was interesting to see the different contexts. The first session was normally about myself as a performer and Dave (my piano accompanist) as a performer, both of us showcasing what we can do. But, ultimately, the goal wasn't just about us performing, but about getting them to replace us so that they took the stage and told their own stories.

Among the people we encountered there was a lady from Nigeria. We were in this church that was empty – a beautiful building. She sang a song in a Nigerian dialect that I could not understand. It was an interesting thing to experience, the shoe on the other foot, because normally, when

I sing in Zulu, people don't understand me. So, it was nice to be the one who did not understand the lyric, for a change, but I could totally get the emotion, mood and the tone behind her story in song.

Another example was when we walked into an entirely different context. After leaving a church where a non-religious Nigerian song was performed for us, we went to a care home and were shown into this room of people who were interested in singing church songs. It was more of a spiritual thing. One gentleman who was quiet and still became really animated when we asked him about his favourite music. He came to life and started singing in this alluring voice with such compelling character. He sang a jazz standard. And then there was also a lady who was singing in Punjabi. Although she couldn't understand English, when somebody translated the key words: 'lullaby' and 'the songs you sang growing up', she started singing. And it was so surreal to see the contrast between European music and these micro tonal Punjabi scales that she was singing.

Eventually, we found, I'll say, a grandma – a beautiful soul – who started singing another song. It took me back to the days when I used to go to church and everything there was based on the minor pentatonic scale. We sang in that scale and the blues scale, too, you know, we preached and breathed in this scale – everything was there. The beautiful thing about her song was that it was repetitive but when you kept on singing that same line, it's like you could see her journey and the things she went through and what the song meant to her.

And that was the beautiful thing about gospel music in the townships, I guess. We did not have overhead projectors, we could not afford to have a lot of lyrics, so the lyrics were repetitive. But then it challenged you as a performer, to make sure that your audience was engaged. So, it forced or rather created an environment that actually encouraged the soloist to start embellishing and enhancing the melody; to improvise by infusing their own story into the song. So, the grandma never sang the same thing twice, you know, and her vocal delivery was amazing.

That project, called the People's Lullabies, seemed to be customised for each and every individual who was involved to tell their own stories. It culminated in the screening of all these lullabies on the big screen at Everyman Cinema in Trinity in Leeds. To sit there and watch it all on the big screen: an Irish lullaby, the Nigerian song, the gospel songs. It was satisfying to see all these people prioritise the story and the message using music as a conduit to tell those stories, even when they were initially apprehensive: 'We are not professionals' they had said. They were now in a place where they could tell their stories from a position of comfort. They could actually sing and they got every note right when they focused on their stories instead of their fears. More importantly, the aesthetic of the song felt so authentic, so real and so genuine and that was a beautiful thing about the project.

Erin Moriarty

I want to think about something that recurred as a theme today – how do we really listen to people who are strangers to us? And I feel like there's also a converse theme of what's the ethics of listening? What's the morality of representing others and especially strangers? And what does it mean to interpret or translate for them? And what does it mean to be interpreted or translated? And I want to talk about the duality of those and really understanding that translation is more out of time; it's asynchronous. It's traditionally linked with literature or screen studies – those sorts of things. Interpretation being much more in the moment, in the now, the transformative encounter.

I wanted to hold those thoughts and then to think about what it means to then have all the different encounters that we've discussed today. And in these encounters, where and when people have different trajectories, different biographies and understandings, what happens when those come together?

Sophie Herxheimer

I think that all any of us want is to be listened to. I think if I do my job properly, I give the person my attention. And I weave around them a sort of sense of safety and insight and they know that they're with me and that I'm not judging them. I don't have time to judge them. I don't have the inclination, but I don't have the time because it's a very quick turnaround. And I think that helps in that people suddenly feel that they could open up, tell me something – and I hope they don't feel robbed, which is why I want to give them a copy of their story.

Sometimes, I say to them, 'Are you okay? Do you want me to share this or not share the story?'. And if they say, 'I can't believe I told you that, please never tell anyone else', then I don't, and I don't share the drawing. There are little bits, a few little rules at the beginning and end of story collecting. Obviously, I don't want it to be an exploitative act. And it is an act in which I am the drawer and I am the artist. But because I've never really enjoyed that idea of the separation of the roles and the punter situation and the expert, I don't really like that, and I find it uncomfortable. Although I don't mind discomfort and I think discomfort is great, because it usually involves something shifting, there's a transformation going on.

Another person, another poet who's been helpful, said to me, 'For every 10 stories you collect from other people, do you collect 10 from yourself? Collect three from yourself'. And I've started doing this. Because I agree that I have a lot of stories. It's a very fluid act and it affects people differently; it affects me differently. It's true that sometimes people haven't been listened to, ever; or they might not have been listened to for some time.

> What is the role of literature in staging these encounters?
> Can it serve as a troubling factor that disturbs the overwhelm-
> ing normative force of the Memory Theatre that demands
> that all encounters be harmonious? And I hope that it can; it
> can disrupt; it can be problematic.

Helen Finch

I'm just going to give you one example of a survivor called Edgar
Hilsenrath who was born in Germany in the 1920s and died only very
recently. He wrote novels throughout the latter half of the 20th century,
brilliant novels, speaking about various aspects of the experience of German Jews not only during the period of the Shoah but also before it – the
period of Jewish culture and Shtetl life, prior to the Second World War –
that was different and that has been irrevocably lost. But also this crucial
experience of the survivor who tries to return to German culture, who
tries to speak in German to a member of the German majority culture,
about a history that the persecutor wishes to forget. I'm going to take
his last novel *Berlin: End of the Line* which was published in 2006 and
stages this encounter between the survivor and the persecutor in intimate
fashion.

Hilsenrath is a satirical and a grotesque writer and his grotesque
writing breaks through the veil of piety with which this German Jewish
encounter is often cloaked. The theorist Max Czollek has spoken of
this as a Theatre of Memory that German majority culture, mainstream
culture, loves certain performances of contrition and restitution through,
for example, constructing memorials such as the memorial to the
murdered Jews of Europe in Berlin. But that actually engaging with the
needs and the histories of real living Jewish people is sometimes a step
too much because they break with the idea of the Memory Theatre in
which everyone knows their predestined role.[7] And Hilsenrath is one
of these people with no interest in the memory theatre in which Jews
encounter Germans only to absolve them of the past, only to talk about
a shared future, only to talk about how much progress Germany has
made since 1945. By contrast, the encounters between German and Jew
in Hilsenrath's work right through the 1950s, 1960s, 1970s and into
this century show and relate encounters that are difficult, that are over-
determined, that are emotional.

And my question then is what is the role of literature in staging these
encounters? Can it serve as a troubling factor that disturbs the overwhelming normative force of the Memory Theatre that demands that all
encounters be harmonious? And I hope that it can; it can disrupt; it can
be problematic.

Charlotta Palmstierna Einarsson

These presentations do not have their meanings determined in advance. The poetic stage images in Beckett's drama therefore seem dependent on the techniques that produce them. For example, isolation, stasis, fragmentation, disappearance. And they also have the power to become significant in many different ways. Not what mismovements mean then, but their potential for becoming meaning is what I have been trying to address. Structurally, Beckett's drama is characterised by incompleteness. It does not tell us what to understand or think. It's not didactic – at least not in any conventional sense of the word. Rather, it invites spectators to pay attention to aesthetic aspects of performance – for instance, shapes and sounds – and to engage imaginatively and creatively in thinking from such experiences. In Beckett's own words, his drama is 'a poetry of the theatre rather than a poetry in the theatre'.

Meaning in this context depends less on whether or not we are able to decode stage images and more on our ability to tune to their appearing as open-ended and ambiguous poetic manifestations. Because clearly we cannot stop making meaning and the crisis of interpretation in Beckett's drama therefore does not do away with meaning; it merely underwrites our complicity and participation in creating it.

Yet, Beckett's drama does not tell us what to understand or think nor does it explain our lives. Rather, it presents an open-ended invitation to participate in the construction of meaning. In other words, Beckett's drama seems to offer up a range of embodied experiences to be imaginatively inhabited by spectators. In so doing, it not only resists habitual or conventional meaning making but it also invites us to look for meaning elsewhere; to attend to what Gendlin terms our felt sense. And to proceed to think from there – from not knowing, from frustration or curiosity, from effect.

I would therefore want to suggest that Beckett's drama unveils the pluralism intrinsic to experience. It invites us to re-evaluate the experience of not only what it means to know something but also what it means to be ignorant, to experience conflict, difference and stuckness. And this, finally, is also how it is ethical. It prompts us to think differently. Because just as dancers often come to realise that injuries are guides not adversaries – guides that help them move differently – we need to dare to let go of what we are most committed to, namely our beliefs and convictions, in order to find routes or ways of communicating with each other. Indeed, as Timothy Garton Ash reminds us, our survival as a species may hinge on our capacity to recalibrate a 'we' in this respect. Thus, finally, may we also come to understand why encountering the other could be so fruitfully conceived in terms of an ethical drama.

Erin Moriarty

Deaf people have different ways of making and enjoying music. I am deaf and don't understand the lyrics of songs but I like the feel of music. I do like the vibration. Lyrics don't mean anything to me, so I experience music in a very different way. But it got me to thinking that – I think somebody else was saying that – music is the translation of the soul. You're putting feelings into sonic vibrations. This made me think about the aesthetics of music and the ways that music is visual and tactile. Here, I will show you some examples of what I mean by visual music.

[Plays a clip of moving waves]

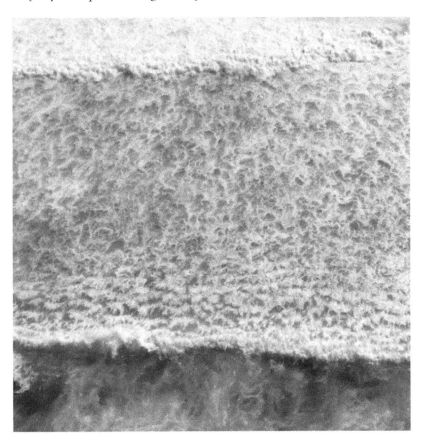

Still image of visual music – moving waves (Erin Moriarty, 2022)

This is a silent video, and you are drawn into the rhythm of the waves. This video is from Bali that I made during fieldwork. This is from an afternoon when I was following a tour group and we were at a crowded tourist site, with masses of people teeming around. I needed a moment of quietness. As I looked down from the cliffs of a Balinese temple in contemplation, I thought, 'There's something intrinsically beautiful in this movement of the water'. As I stood there in silence, focused on the waves, I made the video as a way of focusing on the moment, transcending the chaos behind me. The different sounds, the vibrations, what's happening in reality in terms of the natural world, and then there's something transcendental.

[plays clip of tree blowing in the wind]

Still image of visual music – tree blowing in the wind (Erin Moriarty, 2022)

This clip is of a tree in my backyard. I'm sure most of you can hear when trees rustle in the wind like that and have a different experience than I do. The branches moving in the wind and the slight swaying of the tree is a form of visual music, and this is what I would say is visual music.

Now another example of visual music is this. I don't know if you will be able to understand the meaning of this clip without context but there are two interpreters in the clip. One is a hearing interpreter, one is a deaf interpreter and this is a group of disabled people who came together in Lafayette Square, directly north of the White House, to protest the murders of young Black men in the United States. This was during the Black Lives Matter protests in Washington, DC, after George Floyd's murder by the Minneapolis police. This group includes people in wheelchairs and deaf people, all sorts of disabled people, all who are strangers who have come together, in their anger. This coalition of people have gathered in front of Lafayette Square, which had been fenced off by order of the White House, for a common purpose, united by their anger. This is an example of a visual music of encounter between people united by a common purpose:

[Plays clip of protesters signing in American Sign Language]

Still image of visual music – Black Lives Matter protesters signing in American Sign Language (Erin Moriarty, 2020)

These protesters, some of whom most likely just learned these signs, are signing GF, George Floyd, George Floyd in American Sign Language (ASL). It is a commemoration of his name and his life in ASL. As these disabled people, both deaf and hearing, sign in ASL, it becomes an aesthetic protest, with the visuality of the rhythmic signing by a coalition of disabled people, in wheelchairs and on crutches. You can't help but stare at the different aesthetics here, which creates a feeling of what I think of as productive discomfort.

This sense of discomfort, where the video is silent with a noisy visual aesthetic, can be productive as the viewer, who may not know ASL, is trying to understand what is going on.

Notes

(1) Koch, A., Brierley, C., Maslin, M.A. and Lewis, S.L (2019) Earth system impacts of the European arrival and great dying in the Americas after 1492. *Quaternary Science Reviews* 207, 13–36.

(2) Lewis, S. and Maslin, M. (2015) Anthropocene began with species exchange between old and new Worlds. See https://theconversation.com/anthropocene-began-with-species-exchange-between-old-and-new-worlds-38674 (accessed 28 April 2023).

(3) *Équipée* was first published posthumously, by Plon, in 1929. For its English translation by Natasha Lehrer, see *Journey to the Land of the Real* (2017, Atlas Press).

(4) Pratt, M.L. (1992) *Imperial Eyes: Travel Writing and Transculturation*. Routledge.

(5) Wynter, S. (2003) Unsettling the coloniality of being/power/truth/freedom: Towards the human, after man, its overrepresentation—An argument. *The New Centennial Review* 3 (3), 257–337.

(6) Lugones, M. (2003) *Pilgrimages/Peregrinajes. Theorizing Coalition Against Multiple Oppressions.* Rowman and Littlefield.

(7) Czollek, M. (2023) *Versöhnungstheater (Theatre of Reconciliation).* Carl Hanser Verlag.

4 Negotiating Discomfort Together

A Whole Big Mess – Molly Goehring / Davina De Beer – Lacuna Festivals Clash 2022

Attending to Discomfort

> Being passionate about issues of oppression and privilege
> didn't absolve me from my biases. I had to become comfort-
> able with not always knowing the correct thing to say or do.

Parinita Shetty

In many instances, I'm a part of the dominant culture. Even though I
suddenly became a person of colour when I moved from India to the UK,
this newly-marginalised identity still intersects with a lot of privileges.
I'm in a university space, English is my first language, I grew up with
Western media and culture – and that puts me in a place of privilege. And
while talking to people from all these different cultures in the framework
of my PhD fan/research podcast, I realised how much I didn't know
about people's different identities.

I recorded a total of 22 episodes with participants from diverse
backgrounds. I was frequently self-conscious about my ignorance of
certain identities. In the beginning, I worried about saying the wrong
thing, accidentally offending somebody, especially when we were talking
about a culture that I didn't know really well. Even though I believed I
was open-minded, progressive and inclusive, my project highlighted how
ignorant I was about so many aspects of people's experiences. Being passionate about issues of oppression and privilege didn't absolve me from
my biases. As a cisgender, heterosexual and able-bodied woman, my
dominant culture blind spots especially came to the fore while chatting
with queer and disabled co-participants. Their experiences helped me
understand perspectives that I hadn't encountered before.

I think the way that we challenged each other's perspectives helped
me learn about how much I don't know and that encouraged me to go
and fill in the gaps in my knowledge. I had to become comfortable with
not always knowing the correct thing to say or do. Eventually, I realised
how much I enjoyed being uncomfortable. I don't know if 'enjoyed' is
the correct term, but I really valued the discomfort because I thought it
opened up so many more learning opportunities than if I had just been
comfortable all the time. Sometimes, I changed my mind, sometimes
they did, and other times nobody did; but it was just nice to be able to
unlearn some of the things that I hadn't even realised I took for granted
before.

According to Jake Burdick and Jennifer A. Sandlin's framework 'a
methodology of discomfort',[1] this imperfection is a crucial part of our
knowledge-making process. If I'm one hundred percent comfortable with
all my beliefs, it's likely that I'll overlook the many lives and experiences
I'm wholly ignorant of. Being comfortable with being uncomfortable is
a great way to learn what I don't know. My uncertainty and mistakes
helped me question my assumptions, reflect on my limitations and

exposed me to unexpected ideas, thereby expanding my imagination. I'm still very ignorant about many identities. Although I'm learning to fill in those gaps, the most valuable thing I've found is the discovery of how little I actually do know; how limited my own very specifically situated experiences are. This doubt allows me to seek out more information and stories. This not-knowing is quite liberating.

Kate Fellows

So, what happens when creating a space for different people to come together is not so good, when it's really truly awful? The difference can take many forms – the physical, the emotional and that of opportunity. The opportunity-related ones can be the hardest to see and to recognise and therefore to do something about.

I have very few professional regrets but one I do have involves a young woman who I feel I failed. In a previous role, I was running a summer art school with a group of secondary pupils from what would be termed 'schools in disadvantaged postcodes'. I have a problem with that label too. For me, it was about access to art and to artists, about opening up opportunities for these students. Each school put forward a student who they thought would benefit the most from that experience. When they arrived at the summer school, there was one young woman who didn't look comfortable, happy or excited to be there; very different to the other students I suppose you could say, very different in her approach to the summer school.

Let's call her Emma. Emma perceived the other students as posh; the other students perceived her as from the wrong side of town. No one said anything but you could just sense it was in the room. I was pretty early on in my career, so I tried every tool I knew how to do team building, starting conversations, asking questions, working one to one. But nothing seemed to work. Whatever I did, I hadn't created a safe enough space for Emma to thrive, or for the other students to acknowledge that there was something there and move on from that difference. The students and me as the facilitator had successfully 'othered' Emma. I didn't open the topic up, I didn't approach it diplomatically. Emma left halfway through the week.

Now, many of our school programmes at Leeds Museums and Galleries and other museums aim to close the attainment gap between the pupils who 'have' and those who 'have not' and other various societal labels. The gap has grown during the pandemic. We know that pupils with supportive families are more likely to access provisions of all sorts including the arts, and are therefore more likely to succeed in life. We know they're more likely to vote, they're more likely to report better mental and physical health as they grow up. And we talk a lot about developing cultural capital – growing that sense of entitlement and equality of access to arts and culture.

I thought I was doing that with the summer school but I really wasn't. I was offering another opportunity for those who were supported by their teachers who put them forward and their families who agreed for them to come. I was creating a false sense of access and equality. I was structurally complicit in the act of 'othering'. Emma's parting comment has really stayed with me over the years. She said, 'my dad doesn't even know I'm here. He thinks art is rubbish. It's all pointless'.

Lara-Stephanie Krause-Alzaidi

One day, after the Black Lives Matter (BLM) protests reached Leipzig in East Germany, I took a walk with my husband. We saw a sign that said 'I understand that I will never understand but I stand with you' leaning against a building and that sparked a very interesting conversation between the two of us. And I took one question away that hasn't really left me since then: What is this slogan actually doing here in Leipzig, in Germany?

So I started investigating that by following the slogan through the German web – hashtag or however people were using it – and I found some interesting cases of organisations or individuals using the slogan. I started contacting some people and this is also how I found some of my later interview partners – some black Germans and some white Germans.

In these interviews, I actually wanted to see how people would engage with different slogans that popped up in BLM protests in Germany. I gave them a selection and we talked about them in particular ways. We were guided by the slogans. And something that happened during two interviews was really instructive for me.

During my first interview with Sarah,[2] a black German, I asked her, 'So would you say that Germans would actually have to become white first in the sense that they would have to become conscious of their whiteness so that they can understand?'. And then Sarah interrupted me, saying, 'I wouldn't say Germans because I'm also German'. And that was a moment where I was quite embarrassed, but we moved on and had a very interesting conversation about this.

And because of that I thought, okay I'm going to ask a similar question again, I'm just going to ask it better in the next interview. And a week later in my second interview with Noëmi, also a black German, I had the same slip again and I asked her, 'Would that mean that Germans would have to actually become white first?'. And she said, 'So first I have to correct you because it is already problematic to say that Germans have to first, because I'm also German'. I reacted, 'Sorry I mean the majority population'. And she said, 'Yes, I know how you mean it but that is the interesting thing; that first we have in our head that being German and being white are tied together. All this has stopped being the case ages ago'.

Jonathan Dove

It seemed like such a good idea, to write a piece of music which would tell the true story of a refugee's journey to this country. Why was it proving so hard? Why was it taking so long to find refugees who were prepared to talk about their journey?

In the end, we realised that it might be a very long time (if ever) before any of them was ready to talk in detail about what forced them from their homeland and compelled them to come here. As someone used to listening, and often thought of as sensitive, it was sobering to confront the shortcomings of my imagination.

Awad Ibrahim

Buber[3] makes a distinction between what he calls three types of dialogue. The first is what he calls genuine dialogue. This is where each of the participants really has in mind the other or others with the intention of establishing a living mutual relationship.

The second type of dialogue is what he calls technical dialogue. This is one which is prompted by the need for objective understanding. So, I'm relating to you simply because I want to understand you, and you see this a lot in the classic notion of research. So, we want to just go in in an almost colonial way – you go in and you simply get the information and then you leave.

The third dialogue is what he calls monologue disguised in dialogue. This is one in which two or more people are meeting in space, speaking to each other in strangely torturous ways and yet imagine they have escaped the torment of being thrown back on their own resources. The monologue disguises dialogue. This is the process of echoing. I'm only really hearing my own echo.

This forces us to think about both dialogue and relationship in a different way. Buber calls it the 'I–thou' ethical relationship, as opposed to the 'I–it' relationship. The 'it' is where the other becomes something that is just an object. The 'I–thou', in contrast, is when you move away from the other as an object to other as pure humanity. This relationship becomes an act of love. And this is the ethics that I want us to think about.

Jonathan Dove

Thank you so much for your provocation which I found very beautiful and elegant, and also thank you for introducing me, and perhaps others, to the work of Martin Buber. It was completely new to me. But I now do have *Between Man and Man* on my Kindle and look forward to exploring it in depth later on.

As a musician, I often work with other people's stories, and it's a privilege to be able to give voice to stories that might not get heard, and to help somebody to sing. I sing through others; I create music that somebody else will sing but I'm inspired by someone else's story. And that always seems something to be happy about, and to enjoy being able to help someone else to be heard. But in this particular experience that I was describing in my provocation, there was something painful about realising that one could enter into what I thought of a kind of dialogue, but realised retrospectively that perhaps it was not a genuine dialogue. I find your distinction and Martin Buber's distinction between these different kinds of dialogue very helpful. And I suddenly thought, 'Oh gosh, were we doing – was this a technical dialogue in fact? Was this what was happening?'.

The original impulse for creating this piece of work was, as I say, to share perhaps an archetypal story of a refugee, which I feel is a universal story. Curiously, it was in fact the arts organisation that had the desire to not only engage but also, I suppose, to be seen to engage with its community in a particular way. And so this led to that encounter. And I'm thinking, when an arts organisation approaches refugees to tell their stories, are we really just…? We were entering this dialogue with an objective, we want to come in and get something. And we think, 'well, that is a good thing that we're doing. There's going to be a lovely outcome. It's going to be a beautiful thing'. But has it really emerged as a genuine dialogue?

> These kinds of little, tiny moments of mistrust or miscommunication, do they show the need to focus on the broader perspective?

Sarah-Jane Mason

In 2020, the Lacuna Festival events expanded this interactive way of encountering difference and included 'May We Collaborate', a project where 30 artists from around the world swapped incomplete artworks and finished another artist's work, often encountering a different medium or approach than they were familiar with. Participant feedback from May We Collaborate indicated a strong sense of encountering and meaningfully engaging with difference.

Unfortunately, not all participating artists had a positive experience with the May We Collaborate project. This reminded us of the reality of working with others; you put yourself out there and there is a risk. Trust is given, and if it is broken, it can be hurtful and potentially harmful for encouraging further interactions with difference.

It was absolutely disappointing. My collaborator never delivered work. He or she should have been taken out of the project. It is a total lack of professionalism if you think you can do whatever, whenever you like to. It will come back to you in the end.

This feedback prompted huge reflections for Simon Turner and me at Lacuna Festivals. As facilitators, what role do we have in managing expectations, enforcing promised actions or implementing sanctions? Is it possible to maintain a flat hierarchy within the event and the festival community and to simultaneously hold the responsibilities of others? How can we further support participants in successfully encountering and working with difference?

This holding of responsibility and knowing whose responsibility it is, how you navigate when you're there but you're not meant to be there (because as a facilitator you're almost a silent partner) – in my experience of the events with the festivals, it's really difficult; and it seems like whatever kind of a call I make, it's likely to be the wrong one – it's like I've not found the right balance yet, to get that kind of neutrality. I had to grapple with the feeling of 'it's really familiar but completely strange at the same time'; and how to bridge those gaps where there were miscommunications in moments when we might have a limited time or a particular structure, but something hasn't quite worked in the interpretation, in the communication.

It made me think back to when I was part of an art research project in Brazil,[4,5] with artists from the UK, Brazil and Mexico, and we had four languages and simultaneous interpretation; there were so many issues of how much of yourself is the interpreter able to put across; how do you give your trust to the interpreter to do that, giving yourself up to the process and trusting that it's going to happen. These kinds of little, tiny moments of mistrust or miscommunication, do they show the need to focus on the broader perspective? This is similar to the way that participants work in Lacuna Festivals – there's lots of moments of discomfort of maybe being misrepresented or not being communicated properly. Sometimes, I feel like I have to step in, but I resist because I know it's going to disrupt and it's actually not going to help things.

Charlotta Palmstierna Einarsson

It would appear that a practice-oriented perspective has a lot to offer in this context. Beginning with interaction first affords a different perspective on the ethical drama of encountering the other since it locates the responsibility and accountability for othering in the very process of negotiating experience.

The complexity of experience means that there is always something we don't see, and this awareness seems key not merely to finding out truth but to taking up an ethical stance towards the other.

Facing Realities of Conflict

Ana Deumert

I cited James Baldwin earlier and that maybe links also to the question of the canon and the question of imagining a southern decolonial canon. For me, my inspiration is coming increasingly out of what Cedric Robinson[6] called the Black radical tradition – whether it's African-American thought, Caribbean thought, African thought – and that enormous richness which is there. Especially in African-American thinking, love has been an important concept and Samy Alim uses the concept of loving critique, which is a very interesting concept, also in the context of encounters, particularly among comrades.

Because, although we might agree on the big vision of the society we are working for, we nevertheless have disagreements and, of course, there are conflicts. And so, the concept of loving critique allows us to formulate critiques of each other without entering into conflict. And, I think, that's also where love can be a very powerful moment because disagreements and different views will always be there, and we have to find ways for articulating them. And sometimes it's very difficult, especially with comrades, but maybe it's also easier with comrades because we've got that love for each other.

Irene Heidt

The talk was so broad and it brought up so many ideas I've been pondering throughout the last few years. And I got stuck a little bit with your idea when you refer to Johannes Fabian, and his idea of Gleichzeitigkeit and that theories of intercultural encounter tend to place the other in a different timescale to create a difference between the two. And then there is the sociolinguist Jan Blommaert[7] who has actually argued that there's also a danger in synchronising different time zones into one, because then we erase the face of the other and the historicity of the other. And so, I see a paradox in here.

Also, as far as I understood Levinas[8,9] and his other-oriented ethics, he made the difference between Auffassen and Fassen – to apprehend and to grasp. So, I feel that it's important to see the other in her own timescale, and then to see how that relates or disrelates to where I'm standing, or in other words, to my own times. But maybe I misunderstood you. So, I wanted to hear your thoughts on this paradox or this disrelation between Fabian and the issue of synchronisation.

Gert Biesta

For me, when you use this notion of synchronisation that sort of suggests, let's forget about all the differences and just assume that we're all here together and I think that's naive and dangerous as well. I don't think that this word, that's not what I read there. For me, this idea to become contemporary or Gleichzeitigkeit is not to become identical but to say we are sort of in the same time and we are facing something together. And maybe it links to the question of solidarity where you say we go on the journey together.

The movement to become contemporaries is to say, okay I faced the same issues as you are facing and the way in which we also faced them differently. And I think the word solidarity is really relevant there because you can say, 'what is there for me to do if I try to step in the same time as where you find yourself?'. So, there is something there that is not about just saying we are experiencing things the same or we are the same. I come back to the word solidarity because that helps me to see what's there in trying to be Gleichzeitigkeit. And for me, all these questions always turn back to me. So, it's far less about what others think and what their ideas are but what is there for me to do in that.

I was thinking because I saw your provocation and it's interesting when you get something like different views about homosexuality in the classroom, for example, what do you do with that? Do you frame that as saying, 'oh they have views and they are different from mine' or 'yeah, we were there 20 years ago but we are now here'? Or can you turn that around and say, 'okay there were these different views and opinions and they have their history and their location. But what do I do encountering all that?'.

And for me, that's also an interesting educational move to put a different question back to your students; not which value should you adopt or which ideas should you have and which ideas are you no longer allowed to have. But okay, given that this is the reality, what do you do? Then you come into a different temporal relationship.

Irene Heidt

Yes, I can relate to that but I think it's difficult to become contemporaries so to become people of the same time because we might run the risk of erasing or glossing over differences and contradictions when encountering the other instead of engaging with these differences. This is the distinction Levinas makes between apprehending and grasping the other. To my mind, synchronisation of different timescales and historicities might suggest clarity and cohesion but, as Jan Blommaert (2005: 136)[10] has argued, it is also 'a denial of the complexity of the particular position from which one speaks, and of the differences between that position and that of others'. The challenge then is to understand the other without effacing them, that is, denying the fundamental differences under claims of solidarity. Ultimately, this is the ethical challenge the teacher faces in my provocation. I think I'm viewing things from a different theoretical standpoint but I am very thankful for your thoughts and perspectives.

Erin Moriarty

My PhD research involved fieldwork with deaf people in Cambodia. So, I have that experience of encountering the other, who are also like me in terms of our shared lived experiences of being deaf. Certainly, I can't represent deaf Cambodians because I have a very different positionality from them. I'm a white, deaf woman with all the privileges that come with having an American passport, an American education. So again, of course, this is where you have to work, despite your own comfort levels, at introspection, at reflexivity. I was a little uncomfortable with how many people would congratulate interpreters there, and in many other situations. And sometimes it becomes more about the interpreters or the mediators, the go-betweens than the actual people themselves. And I think that's problematic. And it's important that we look at those tensions and consider those tensions in such encounters.

Amber Galloway-Gallego

How music has connected me to the deaf world happened well over 20 years ago. I would host parties at my house, and all my deaf and hard of hearing friends would come over, and we would take turns signing songs, dancing, acting the fool. But it always centred around music and signing; it was just part of our regular Friday night activities. Then, one night I was fortunate enough to attend an event hosted by the San Antonio deaf dance company, and it was at this performance that I witnessed greatness that would change the way I saw music interpreting forever. I sat back and watched these phenomenal dancers, The Wild Zappers, a deaf dance group, incorporate music with signs, and I knew that this is what signing music should look like when we were interpreting.

I began utilising these concepts based on what I saw The Wild Zappers do and what my deaf friends said they wanted to see on stage. I was able to do it and had been doing it year after year. It was awesome to see the request for music interpreting increase significantly during these times. An interesting turn of events occurred in the earlier part of my interpreting career. While I was working, I contracted spinal meningitis, which contributed to me losing 50% of my hearing, changing the trajectory of my life – not only shifting my identity but strengthening my understanding of the deaf and hard of hearing world. I began to experience several of the same barriers to communication as my deaf and hard of hearing friends had experienced since birth.

My first trip abroad was to Norway. I hosted an intense music workshop for a group of interpreters. One of the interpreters was a deaf interpreter from Denmark. She explained her love for music and how she wanted to be a music interpreter, but she was told by hearing people that this was not possible. I assisted her in changing that narrative and look at this incredible work.

I was then invited to Switzerland. I hosted an event for the deaf community as well as for the hearing community to show them my work and also explain the importance of providing access to music. It was an incredible night. Then, I was off to the Czech Republic where I was invited to interpret on stage at a major music festival and they told me that this was the first time that this had ever happened in the country. I was also asked to be a speaker at that same festival, and I was lucky enough to team up with a group called Hands Dance which is a performing troupe of deaf and hearing interpreters.

A year later, I was able to take my team of interpreters to Ukraine to teach music interpreting. We provided in-depth training to interpreters and prepared them for a large music festival that we would all be working at. During this process, I noticed a couple of deaf people observing the training. They expressed their interest in interpreting music, but many had told them it was not possible. So, I helped them rewrite their narrative and invited them to work the music festival as well.

The last country I went to before our world was changed by the pandemic was Romania. Leading up to the festival, I was able to train the interpreters virtually for a few months prior to the actual event. I had also met a deaf person who wanted to be a part of this experience. She told me that many of her colleagues said that deaf people cannot interpret music and I emphatically disagreed with them. I showed the hearing interpreters several videos of deaf interpreters on my team who interpret at music events in the States. They were shocked but it also helped them realise to not put limits on anyone. At the festival, I was able to bring one of the Ukrainian deaf interpreters to help assist and support the Romanian deaf interpreter. For the first time in her country, Elizabeta, a deaf interpreter, was onstage at a major music festival, and it was a historic experience for so many of us. There were over 200 deaf people in attendance.

Erin Moriarty

I just really wanted to say and emphasise how big a difference there is in the embodied experience of people who are born deaf and who grew up deaf from people who become deaf later in life, as well as people who have partial hearing and/or speaking skills. It is important to emphasise that there is a spectrum of experiences across these groups. And there's always a tangent about who speaks for whom in parts of the community, the whole of the community.

So, I just want to signal that it's terrific to see this work out in the world visible, and to see discussions about it. But, I thought it important that people who don't understand a lot of these politics understand that the positionality of sign language interpreters in terms of say signing on the platform or on the stage is a vexed issue in our community. And there are many different points of view and it's important to bear that in mind.

Charlotta Palmstierna Einarsson

The divisions that open up in discourses – for example on climate, gender, inequality, religion – signal the need to come together to reflect on the problems we share because we should never forget that others too share in our concerns. We mustn't believe that those who do not agree with us fail to see the world as it is or that they do not understand the nature of the problem.

As Stanley Cavell reminds us, 'the wish and search for community are the wish and search for reason'.[11] Signalling one's belonging to a group then entails constructing identity through conventional patterns of communication, and as such it is an important aspect of our collective intentionality. Yet, such thinking alike is also what produces othering. In light of this, it seems appropriate to remind oneself that when I present an idea that doesn't resonate with anyone, the problem may not be that the idea is invalid; it may merely be that I'm appealing to the wrong group.

Yet, as Barad reminds us, we might also want to ask, 'what if we were to recognise that differentiating is a material act that is not about radical separation but on the contrary about making connections and commitments?'.[12] Would such an understanding of differentiating change our understanding of self and other?

It is a little bit like when we were kids and our parents told us that we couldn't swear ourselves free from the responsibility of being there or participating in an argument, sharing and making connections, even as those connections appeared as divisions. It is an ethical stance to acknowledge this: whether we disagree or agree, we are bound together.

Gert Biesta

Often, encounters are surprises that are beyond our control. When you step into the encounter, all of these things, like empathy, respect, tolerance, sensitivity, flexibility, may be there or may not be there. So, there is the real question of whether these lists that are sort of circulated in education actually speak to the reality of the encounter. The other question that I find urgent, but also difficult, is that I am not sure whether everyone deserves my empathy, respect, tolerance, sensitivity and flexibility.

Ana Deumert

I was also thinking about something else, namely that I'm not sure that my love and willingness to include is boundless. Are there limits to inclusion? And I'm thinking here of my own work on whiteness and racism. I was taking my cue from Steve Bantu Biko and attempted to do this work to unmask whiteness and white supremacy, as part of an anti-racist politics. Yet, to study far-right spaces – and my work was focused on digital worlds – killed me inside. I would end my days in disgust and anger unable to communicate, even with those closest to me. Do I wish for dialogue? Do I wish to engage in acts of inclusion? Is there an art to hearing the racist, sexist, homophobic, xenophobic other?

In their proposal, Maggie and Angela speak about a coarsening of the public sphere, and this is one very visible part of it. Reflecting on this, I was reminded of Pumla Gobodo-Madikizela's book *A Human Being Died That Night*.[13] In the book, she writes about her interviews with the state-sanctioned apartheid mass murderer Eugene De Kock and how she engaged with him, how she struggled in the process, but how she managed to hold him accountable and to forgive him.

What kind of ethical framework can help us in such encounters? Encounters that create a specific form of discomfort or, rather, of disgust. How do we hold responsibility in these spaces and how do we stay true to our political commitments?

Erin Moriarty

I just want to talk about contact zones a little bit because I think there's a really strong metaphorical change in what safe space means because of COVID and the pandemic. Can unsafe spaces be productive is a question that we have to ask ourselves and look at ourselves. What does our discomfort tell us? Is there something to be learned?

> **We still have to have those everyday conversations with the other which may be nothing but they are something. And therefore they continue to be important in moments of conflict.**

Maggie Kubanyiova

Something that I really would love to hear more about is the idea of the limits to encounters. And you touched on a very important topic there. In relation to fraught and difficult encounters, you raised the question of whether they are even possible and do we even want them to happen? I am reminded of a story involving Hilke Wagner, director of the Albertinum Museum in Dresden, who faced a backlash from the right-wing movement by inviting her attackers into the museum. It kind of really opened up that whole debate: do we continue or stop the conversation? If we are clear that we absolutely have limits, then what are the consequences, what does that mean for encounters, what does that mean for us?

Ana Deumert

Yeah, I'm glad you picked up the question because it is not something I really know how to deal with. I know that when I did a paper on the far right in South Africa, writing that paper was emotionally impossible.

I couldn't speak to anyone, I couldn't speak to my partner, because I was just surrounded by filth. I can't say it in any other way. Racist filth. And taking my cue from Steve Biko, as white people, we do need to do the work of transformation, of challenging racism in our own corners, we need to do that. So, that is why actually those conversations are important to have.

But they are incredibly difficult… I mean I think it's just the closeness to it, to encountering the violence. And I don't know. I just know that is my experience and I wonder how I would react if I was in a conversation. Very often, we have affinity networks, friendship networks; where we have solidarity; where we are with political soulmates. For me it's really the question – in encounters, it's all about dialogue, getting to know the other, listening – but there is a line.

Maggie Kubanyiova

Yeah, and I really appreciate the stance of not having the answer.

Angela Creese

Ana, you talked about the importance of overlapping speech as a kind of prosaic everyday phenomenon that perhaps we miss in online worlds. And it seems to me that overlapping speech is also a kind of metaphor for dealing with the difficult and for encounters which are really conflictual. Because I think in the TLANG project,[14] we found that public space was still incredibly important so that we didn't stay in our silos and that we did have to engage with the racist other or somebody that we felt very uncomfortable with. And those kinds of public spaces, of course, are also as we know, politically being closed down.

And while I absolutely understand you saying that that was torturous for you to write up as a paper or to deal with, we can't – as I'm sure you would agree – we don't shut ourselves off from it completely and we have to manage it in those kinds of overlapping speech moments. And so, I think going back to that kind of everyday interaction is really important to still hang on to, even when we're talking about the conflictual and those big political conflicts. We still have to have those everyday conversations with the other, which actually just as in Goffman's terms – they may be nothing but they are something. And therefore, they continue to be important, I think, in moments of conflict.

Rosine Kelz

To encounter the irreducible alterity of another person is to have an, at times unexpected, insight that community or intimacy is limited, that one's own assumptions about the other are fallible. When individuals find that they do not see the world the same way or understand a concept in the same way, and that they can give no reason for why they see or understand it in the way they do, this does not imply that there are no facts. As Cavell writes:

> I recognize that the other must find her own way out of her isolation, as I must. And while words are in such a moment pointless, they have not vanished. They can seem solider than ever.[15]

While people find themselves always already in community with others, the social natures of embodied existence, of language and meaning don't preclude the pervasive possibility of isolation and loneliness. The point is that we need to find a way out of isolation, again and again, thus reaffirming our connection to others and to the world.

Finally, for Cavell, encountering the other teaches us about ourselves as moral beings. We learn about how far we can accommodate difference, and also whether we're able to explain our own responses to ourselves. In the end, what we might learn in such encounters is that we have not just been mistaken about the other, but that we have actually been mistaken about ourselves.

Does it always have to be about generating sameness or could we generate forms of solidarity not based on shared identity? This question has also come up repeatedly in feminist and queer theory and activism: Do 'we' all have to understand ourselves as 'woman' – and agree on a definition of that term – in order to formulate a shared feminist politics? In my view, I do not have to feel or define my 'sameness' with others; my political practice can start by formulating my understanding of solidarity with them.

Charlotta Palmstierna Einarsson

Last week, I Zoomed in on a public defence, because in Sweden a viva is a public affair. The respondent was a Swedish Lutheran priest who had written a thesis on the resilience of the Swedish church. Her study applied systems theory to identify some criteria that could be seen to explain and safeguard the flexibility of the church as a system. Arguably, the idea to use systems theory, and specifically the concept of resilience, to examine how the church is able to survive in the changing world is a thought-provoking move. But the respondent also made a comment at the very end of her defence that struck me as relevant to our discussion about encountering difference.

She said that the church as an institution is a commemorative space, its function being to remind us to doubt our convictions, critique our traditions rather than confirm them, and that this necessary collapse of ideas is what has safeguarded the ethics of encountering the other at the core of religious belief. Consequently, she argued, the resilience of the church depends on its ability to sustain doubt without giving up on its core values. And as I understood it, these values were precisely following John D. Caputo's Theology of Perhaps, that God is a human responsibility open to the unexpected and to risk, and that such an openness is the necessary foundation for an ethics of interpretation.[16]

I found the notion that the church is a commemorative space where difference could be negotiated highly persuasive. Yet, I would want to add that if religion is useful in this respect, then arguably so is education and art across genres. For instance, as Simon Critchley explains, the theatre was once a theatron, a theorisation of practice that presented audiences with the opportunity to engage in, what he calls, adversary reasoning.[17] In a context dominated by war, ancient Greek dramas, according to Critchley, played out opposing views so as to help spectators see the others' perspective; the perhaps that lingers in between self and other, us and them, conviction and doubt. Thus, in Aeschylus's *Agamemnon*, as Marc Barham points out, Agamemnon is caught in a moral dilemma: should he obey the goddess Artemis and sacrifice his daughter Iphigenia, in which case the Greek fleet would be able to sail to Troy and recover Helen. Or should he disobey the goddess and save his daughter, in which case he would be responsible for the Greek failure to bring Helen back. A failure that would also entail failing the god Zeus's loyalty test because Zeus was the god whose authority had been violated by Helen's abduction and whose honour the mission intends to restore.[18]

Agamemnon's dilemma, similar to Abraham's, could be seen to open a route to experience the complexity of truth. Notably, says Critchley, the dilemma presented in Greek tragedy produces a situation in which opposing views are made understandable, and difference to some extent cancelled out or at least undermined. Because, as Critchley says, if every option seems both right and wrong, then what should one do? By means of adversary reasoning, audiences were therefore invited to recognise the validity of perspectives, even if they didn't share in them. And adversary reasoning could perhaps therefore also be seen as an ethical practice. The ancient tragedies negotiate a difference by means of unfolding a multiplicity of perspectives.

Notably, however, as William Connolly points out, any claim to pluralism is not simply a claim about 'a tolerant form of life'.[19] This is not some form of relativism, but rather an invocation to rethink our complicity in producing difference. In other words, we are intrinsically part of the conflicts we seek to solve as well as of the discursive context within which these conflicts are shaped.

So, perhaps getting stuck in between opposing views is not necessarily a bad thing. Indeed, getting stuck may force us to stay with problems, prompt us to dwell in ambiguity, and such dwelling often allows us to see things we didn't see before. Drama and artistic manifestations more broadly afford such opportunities. They prompt us to acknowledge and affirm the potential for being otherwise.

Notes

(1) Burdick, J. and Sandlin, J.A. (2010) Inquiry as answerability: Toward a methodology of discomfort in researching critical public pedagogies. *Qualitative Inquiry* 16 (5), 349–360.
(2) Name has been changed.
(3) Buber, M. (2002) *Between Man and Man*. Routledge.
(4) Potency and Potential of Creative Connections in Interstitial Spaces: Learning from Latin American Perspective. Researchers: Anni Raw (University of Leeds), Hillary Ramsden (University of South Wales) and Victoria Jupp Kina (University of Dundee). Date: 2015–2016.
(5) Raw, A. (2016) 'Potency and potential' in interstitial creative spaces: Transformative spatial practices amongst socially-engaged artist/activists. Dossier Arte, Mundo. Revista NAVA, Federal University of Juiz de Fora.
(6) Robinson, C. (1983/2000) *Black Marxism: The Making of the Black Radical Tradition*. University of North Carolina Press.
(7) Blommaert, J. (2005) *Discourse: A Critical Introduction*. Cambridge University Press.
(8) Levinas, E. (1989) Ethics as first philosophy. In S. Hand (ed.) *The Levinas Reader. Emmanuel Levinas* (pp. 75–88). Blackwell.
(9) Levinas, E. (1991) *Totality and Infinity: An Essay on Exteriority*. Springer Dordrecht.
(10) Blommaert, J. (2005) *Discourse*. Cambridge University Press.
(11) Cavell, S. (1979) *The Claim of Reason: Wittgenstein, Scepticism, Morality, and Tragedy*. Oxford University Press.
(12) Barad, K. (2011) Nature's queer performativity. *Qui Parle* 19 (2), 121–158.
(13) Gobodo-Madikizela, P. (2003) *A Human Being Died That Night: A South African Story of Forgiveness*. Houghton Mifflin Company.
(14) Creese, A. (2018) Translating and translanguaging (TLang). See https://tlang.org.uk/ (accessed 29 April 2023).
(15) Cavell, S. (2005) *Philosophy the Day After Tomorrow* (p. 136). The Belknap Press of Harvard University Press.
(16) Caputo, J. (2013) *The Insistence of God: A Theology of Perhaps*. Indiana University Press.
(17) Critchley, S. (2017) The European Graduate School / EGS. Thursday, 19th October, Valletta, Malta. Public open lecture for the students of the Division of Philosophy, Art & Critical Thought. See https://www.youtube.com/watch?v=2QOMx1kMngo.
(18) Barham, M. (2023) 'The sacrifice of Iphigenia' and Agamemnon's dilemma: In defence of Agamemnon. Unpublished text derived from *Academia*. https://medium.com/counterarts/the-sacrifice-of-iphigenia-and-agamemnon-s-dilemma-1c6de5c3cb35.
(19) Connolly, W. (1995/2004) *The Ethos of Pluralism*. University of Minnesota Press.

5 Making Space for Encountering Difference

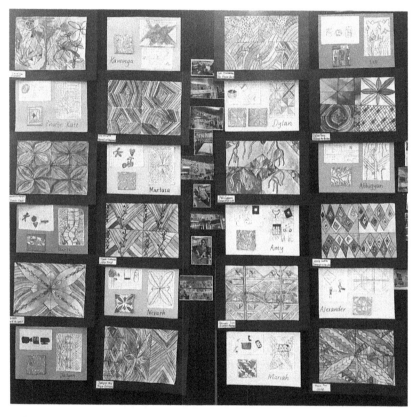

Students' artwork from Sylvia Park School, New Zealand, creating their 'How can we tell our story through visual art?' class project (Photo by Dagmar Dyck, 2021)

Flattening Spatial Hierarchies

The differences of the people involved are not ignored or denied but acknowledged and used to create new experiences that are not just an addition of aspects from both sides.

Cornelia F. Bock

In my PhD thesis, I analyse the interplay of language, religion and identity in a joint German-African church service. This intercultural church service is set in the city of Hamburg; it has been regularly held once a month for several years and it is organised by an African church and a German church. The 'Other' and the encounter with it are highly relevant because of the congregation's composition that includes differences in ethnic, cultural, linguistic and religious background as people from several West African countries, Germans and others come together to worship.

The aim of the service is to facilitate intercultural exchange and to create a sense of community – a new identity shared by both Africans and Germans. The people involved in it are conscious about the fact '[…] that sharing the same space is a necessary but insufficient condition for [meaningful engagement with difference] to occur'.[1]

In my research, I focus on linguistic and other practices that can be identified as aimed at bringing all parishioners together and on how the goal of creating a new community with a shared identity is pursued. The structure of the service as well as interview data clearly show that the basic strategy is not to just line up elements from both traditions but to interweave them in order to create a new joint tradition of worship. One pastor describes it as follows: 'Our demand on the joint service has always been that this is not a German service, this is not a Ghanaian service, but we develop a new shared form and we try to do this with all elements'.

Essential to creating a new shared identity is not to deny differences and the conflicts they might entail, but to acknowledge them and to use them to create new experiences. Participating in the German-African church service means to see, hear and even talk to the 'Other'. This is true not only for the encounter with other people from different backgrounds but also for experiencing liturgical elements that vary from being completely unfamiliar to differing only slightly from one's own experiences. The parishioners need to be open to the new and unknown and be ready to leave their comfort zones in order to be able to engage meaningfully with the 'Other' and start processes of mutual learning. While seeing and hearing the 'Other' are basically part of all liturgical elements, some parts are intended to literally bring all people closer together and to reduce feelings of foreignness.

The differences of the people involved are not ignored or denied but acknowledged and used to create new experiences that are not just an addition of aspects from both sides.

Because of their unique design and execution, the sermons might be the peak of engagement with the 'Other'. The two pastors preach in English and German and draw on their own ethnic, cultural, linguistic and religious backgrounds and individual experiences. This enables everyone to identify with certain aspects and increases the authenticity of the claim of intercultural exchange. The parishioners can, on the one hand, follow familiar aspects such as a familiar language, a familiar style of preaching and a person with a similar cultural background. On the other hand, they can simultaneously experience the 'Other' in a safe space. They are still able to follow the sermon due to the familiar parts and, at the same time, they are not an obvious outsider in this event. Therefore, everyone can feel welcome while still experiencing new and foreign things.

Helen Finch

I was thinking about the relationships of power in the ownership of the church buildings that you described in your fascinating research, Cornelia. And, in particular, the fact that the German Protestant community owned the church buildings and whether that meant that there was some kind of a curatorial relationship with the African churches. Are African congregants seen on the one hand, as you said, disruptive in their worship practices, but also in some way, providing new life or an impetus for European churches that have in some way lost contact with their own original communities? And there's a certain patronising attitude sometimes that 'Africans are the future of our church', 'they are "other" but they're very useful to have'. Maybe that's a little uncharitable. But anyway, I was wondering if you could speak to that a little.

Cornelia F. Bock

Yeah, you're absolutely right. It's often the case in Germany where migrant churches use the buildings that were built for the local churches. It's often just a renting relationship, basically, where the migrant churches rent the rooms for specific times and are not visible in or outside the church building itself outside those times. So, for example, when looking at posters and announcements, it's often just the German church that you see there, and so you don't even know that there are other events taking place.

And in the case that I'm looking at, it's pretty different because nowadays the church building is only used by the African church and another Ghanaian church. The German Protestant worship service is taking place in another church. They had used two buildings, but now they're only using one. So, this church and the whole premises and the office spaces and everything are only used by the African church and the pastor is also hired by the Northern German Church Association. So, this is completely a space for the African churches and the events they host. I'm not sure about the financial arrangements, but it's seen as belonging to the African church and completely used by them. So all the posters and announcements that are hung up by them concern their events or joint events, of course. And that's a different case. But it's usually true that migrant churches are not very visible.

Anna Douglas

We can speak at this present moment in time of a sort of crisis in museums. Their European colonial past has really now come to the fore. And many of us working in the art museum sectors have had these disquiets for many decades. But this question of who the museum is for, who they represent, what stories have been told, is now absolutely critical. But what I think I'm struck by is that the actual status of the museum – in its exclusivity, in its so-called elitism, in its status that represents this kind of custodial role in terms of culture and values – can actually be negotiated and appropriated. So while there is this huge drive in the museum sector around inclusivity now, and rightly so, it strikes me that it is the very status that then also becomes something that people want to be part of and acquire.

And certainly in my own work, I've seen this when putting on an exhibition in Manchester that was particularly focusing on working-class culture in 1960s and 1970s Salford. The museum received almost one of the largest attendance figures it's ever had. And it worked precisely against the very status of its elitism. And now the question, of course, is can the museum hold on to that audience, or are they just, in a sense, bespoke? And I think one of the things that struck me about Thea's presentation is this idea that Indigenous peoples actually wanted to be part of it, they wanted a part of this cultural stake. It was significant to them in terms of identity-building, that the very status of the museum recognised their identity status. And I just think this is a fascinating territory of negotiation.

Thea Pitman

So, it was important for the Indigenous people in the project to go to the museum. Some of them were saying 'We have never set foot in a museum before'. Some of them had never been to Salvador, which is their state capital – the equivalent of someone you know in Yorkshire saying I've never been to London. So yes, that was very important. But the project had a flip side which I wasn't showing you, which is that, after the exhibition in Salvador, a travelling exhibition then also took the artworks that were movable, and with an electronic arts exhibition, quite a lot of them could be moved, and it toured the Indigenous communities that had participated. So, it was important also to ensure that a much wider range of community members than could get to Salvador to see the exhibition there could participate in the project.

I've also been tracking all sorts of other exhibitions that have been going on in Brazil that have involved Indigenous art or Indigenous curatorship in some way. And there are, of course, huge tensions about how Indigenous art enters the formal elite art circuit and whether it is consumed in that process, and what you can do to avoid being entirely co-opted by the museums. And because the relationship between the museum and the project that I was involved in was tense and possibly deteriorating, it was at the same time productive because that stand-off allowed that space for contestation.

If the museum starts to co-opt Indigenous presence and performativity too much, then you end up with something rather like a 'human zoo'. This museum was in a media blackout actually because of elections. But it also didn't have a functioning web page, and so it just did not advertise the exhibition, did not advertise the fact that Indigenous people would even be there. So, that gave them the ability to do things in a much more spontaneous fashion. There was no 'At 2.30, there will be a ritual' kind of stuff. And I think it's that negotiation, or lack of negotiation, that challenges the museum and what the museum and its protocols might be, that was important.

Cornelia F. Bock

What stuck with me was the story you told of the Nigerian woman singing a song and you experiencing that you understood the emotion and the tone, the story, she was telling but not the language, not the lyrics and actually that happens in the church as well.

Thandanani Gumede

The People's Lullabies project that included the Nigerian woman was a project by Opera North in Leeds. In the past, they would normally have artists who'd come to perform in the space, then they would ask the artists to sing a lullaby. But that building was under renovation. Therefore, instead of artists coming into the building, they sent me to different places, so that I could sing lullabies to these different people. And in the South African context, a lullaby wasn't just about a mother singing to a child, but a nation singing itself to sleep because of the traumas of the past. So a song like 'Thula Sizwe' means 'Nation, Cry No More'. With my colleague who was a pianist and a composer, we went around to different people. And these audiences would choose one or two people who we then worked with so that they would replace us, and they would sing their lullabies instead of us.

Claiming Space

Sometimes we need space just to be.

Khadijah Ibrahim

My work focuses around marginalised communities, landscape and liminal spaces. It is an idea that I developed during the pandemic that looked at marginalised communities mainly through the African Caribbean lens of art and ancestry. In 2021, I created a performance art installation called My Body is a Protest for Change.

The 20th-century philosopher Theodor Adorno famously wrote that 'all art is an uncommitted crime'. What he meant was simply that it is the very nature of art that challenges the status quo. Throughout history, artists have reacted or re-enacted against oppression, violence, injustice and inequalities. They have stood up for the voiceless and the marginalised communities. Art is also a form of protest; art that challenges traditional boundaries, hierarchies, rules imposed by others in power. My Body is a Protest is really about the way in which we challenge the landscape, buildings and bodies.

When we begin to interrogate art, architecture, bodies and buildings, there is a sense of silence. This performance art installation gathered a number of poets in a space to think about the landscape and the art of silence – the silence that is often around us when we very rarely want to talk about race or racism, or the boundaries set on artists of who can enter a space and who cannot.

Audre Lorde said, 'the revolution is not a one-day event' but Nina Simone's quote is that 'the artist's duty is to reflect the times'. My Body is a Protest for Change was about not only reflecting the times especially through the pandemic but also addressing the past. To enter or re-enter a space of clarity, we often need clarity to know who we are; that we have a right to be in spaces. There are all these institutions that very rarely allow entry to art and expression from black artists or marginalised artists. This aspect of the installation was a silent protest – just being artists in the landscape. Racism often means that we spend a lot of time reacting; sometimes we need space just to be.

Mohasin Ahmed

What really interested me was when you talked about the distance we feel when we look outside ourselves. Because for me, with Mojxmma, I try to create a space because I can quite clearly see the distance between me and others. And then the space that I try to create is to bring people together; to make a space where there is no distance between people and to allow people to feel comfortable and to feel like they can move and take up space when in mainstream society they don't feel that they can take up that space. What does space mean to you and how do you understand distance and space between different groups and identities?

Heather Harrington

As you were creating a space, we see ourselves as more inserting ourselves into this space. This is particular to the stage and dance. Nadra and I are of an age where it's like 'Well, we don't want to see them on the stage'. So we have resisted and disrupted that by saying, 'Well, we're here'. So, in that way, we feel as though we don't want to go outside and create this space, but come in and disrupt and claim our space. Just say, 'I'm here and I will speak'. Even the imagery of having a physical body that is not young – it is an action of defiance on the stage.

Nadra Assaf

Older women are considered more like minor bodies and the younger bodies are the ones that are more assertive and more powerful. I think as I started approaching 50 – which was before Heather did, of course, and I'm 58 now – but I felt like my space was diminishing, that my ability to have a place that I could launch from and speak my voice in the way that I prefer, which is through my body, was diminishing. And so I thought it would be wonderful to have or, using Mohasin's word, create a place for myself. And that's what I thought I was doing.

It wasn't until after Heather and I connected that we realised we weren't really creating a place. We were asserting our place in that space. So, the space is there, but we just don't want to be pushed aside or pushed to the periphery of the space. We still want to be in it and we think we're still valuable and we have a lot to say.

Ana Deumert

There is a very beautiful article by Linda Alcoff, an American philosopher, where she discusses the work of María Lugones.[2] And she talks about the future, where we will be able to dance in the streets, in public spaces. But we will also be able to debate with each other, to deal with conflicts, to deal with disagreements. So, she uses María Lugones's work to articulate this vision, and that actually stayed with me. Because, also again, it was dance – we might not agree with each other and debate with each other, but we dance with each other. So, the artfulness came in again.

> A lot of people will not want to notice but lying down on the sidewalk or crawling on the sidewalk? Someone's going to notice.

Heather Harrington

When talking about creating a space versus inserting oneself into the space, it made me think of protest and the everyday choreography in a space. Bringing me to Heidegger in the sense that we just want to go on with our usual routine; every day is like, 'I don't notice, I need to get to work; I'm just going to go about what I need to do'. And this is the everyday choreography. I was thinking about protest and the insertion of somebody into a site which somehow breaks that everyday choreography by making somebody notice.

My thesis examined political protest dance in the theatre versus bringing the dance out into the public space to people who might not see it. There are a select few who are going to go to the theatre. So many people will not be exposed to the dance because of a variety of divisions in society. But a body coming into the public space and creating a change to the everyday choreography will make someone stop and get out of their normal routine. I think a lot about the public space, inserting and changing the choreography, and being noticed or not; there is an ethics to it. A lot of people will not want to notice, but lying down on the sidewalk or crawling on the sidewalk? Someone's going to notice.

Thea Pitman

In their exhibit at the modern art gallery in Brazil, the Indigenous people broke some of the standard protocols of an art museum, such as selling arts and crafts in the exhibition space. Tawaná Kariri-Xocó was selling maracás and other things while also engaging members of the public with the artwork that he had been involved with. And they were also doing things in a very impromptu manner so that the institution couldn't really co-opt it and use it for its own ends.

In my research, what I've been trying to do is track those interactions between the museum and its positionality with the project and the Indigenous people involved in it. So, of course, the museum had opened its doors to this project, so it's not completely taking the place by storm. It's not that kind of occupation of, you know, 'We've come to demand our funerary urns back', which does also happen in other museums in Brazil. But it had only fractionally opened them and there were tensions throughout.

There were people there, the Indigenous people who came to the event, who commented on the fact that it was held in a deconsecrated chapel on the quay side in Salvador, which is where slaves would have been landed in the past. And so it's a very highly charged cultural space. One person said, 'Yeah, this is kind of uncomfortable'. But on the other hand, it was such a culturally loaded space that the reclaiming of the ability to be in that space was more powerful.

So, what they had actually originally asked to do was to camp out in the space, to sleep there overnight, to fully occupy it. They wanted to have a campfire outside because anything that they do in terms of Indigenous rituals involves a campfire and smoking a pipe to open channels with spirits and so on and so forth. So, there were certain things that they didn't manage to negotiate with the museum. But there were other things where the museum had said no that they managed to do all the same. So eating, drinking and smoking in the exhibition space all took place. But it was the selling of arts and crafts alongside the exhibition of the more 'high art' side of things that I thought was really interesting. That the museum had said 'No. The gift shop is down there by the toilets and that's where that stuff goes', and the Indigenous artists had refused that separation. And the public rose to the challenge as well. People negotiated the complexities of that space.

Thus, the Indigenous people retained control and they retained agency over the way that they were present in the museum. It wasn't so much a 'human zoo' because that's the danger of bringing Indigenous people into spaces where they have not traditionally been – there have been plenty of examples of that. But I think that the impromptu fashion in which they seized the space allowed for them to perform Indigeneity in an un-co-opted way.

Space in the Making

Nigel Rapport

Cosmopolitan politesse is an interactional code by which one addresses the common humanity and the distinct individuality of those one interacts with but classifies them in no more specific fashion.[3,4] One presumes that in the social interaction, one is engaging with an individual human other; someone who might be called *Anyone* and not with a representative of some more substantive class – a woman, a Swede, a Jew, someone working class, heterosexual, pious or so on. A human being, anyone, possesses an intrinsic identity by virtue of their distinct and finite embodiment. Each inhabits a body that affords a unique perspective on the world; a unique capacity for interpreting an environmental world and making it meaningful and a unique history and practice in such individual worldviews.

This is the ontological reality of human individuality. Cosmopolitan politesse seeks to recognise this and give it its proper respect and so to emancipate anyone socially from the tragedy of merely being made subject to the arbitrary constructions, the fictions, of cultural and symbolic classes and categories. A cosmopolitan public space is one of universality where individual human beings meet, engage with and make space for one another. One recognises *Anyone* as an individual human being entrained on a life course amid worldviews of his or her own determination; and one affords the other the space necessary to fulfil personal life-projects to the extent that these do not prejudice the potential fulfilment of anyone else.

Anna Douglas

The first task I set students even before we had collectively exchanged our names was to respond to an instruction I set. In an empty space, you will find 100 large sheets of blank paper, a pair of scissors and a reel of double-sided tape. Please take 20 minutes and cover the floor in whichever way you choose. Having achieved this action, I then invited the students now standing on the paper carpet to reflect on how the space had changed, how did it now look and feel to them. Unequivocally, students found the space different. It felt bounded, primed for action, full of possibility, warmer, friendlier and cleaner. Indeed, with no furniture in the room, no chairs, no tables, students now decided to sit down really quite spontaneously again with no instructions from me.

Sitting on the floor in a circle, we reflected again on what sitting in this space felt like. Some of them said it was reminiscent of primary school, storytime, playing with friends and feeling safe. It was both new and familiar. Sitting like this in this space, having done this activity, was quite evidently prompting the reliving of a memory-based experience of being children. This seemed to have a real releasing effect of creating the space for play. Only after we'd shared these thoughts did we actually share each other's names, so we got to know each other through doing, not by primarily exchanging information about ourselves.

Why did I decide to actually do the action before even exchanging names? I have two friends who are Irish and they had moved from Ireland to Northern Ireland. I remember them once saying to me that the moment they disclose their name, people are already interpreting who and what they are, based on the fact that their names are Gaelic and thus all kinds of assumptions are made. I think that by going straight into the activity of not even exchanging names, I was actually trying to find a way of exchanging something about being together and cooperating with each other. So, in a way, we all become the same. I mean this is also a fiction, because we're not. But actually what I'm trying to do is invent the fictional space where we can actually relate to each other without preconceived ideas about who each other is. That is a fiction, and I do acknowledge it is a fiction.

And, in a way, I was trying to work outside of impossible really – outside of language, outside of too much discussion, outside of too much revealing of oneself. Actually, what I was trying to encourage students to do was just to find their connections with each other through doing. I was also trying to model something which is about the transformation of space. And maybe various people in the panel particularly interested in architecture might appreciate how quickly you can transform a space by doing something as simple as putting paper on a floor, and how the whole of the mode of behaviour for the rest of that session changes dramatically because of that. And what I wanted students to do was to begin to think about how easy it was to do that experientially because they in turn could begin to do the same in their own artistic practices with others.

The United States Capitol building in Washington, DC, behind fences (Erin Moriarty, 2021)

Erin Moriarty

The photograph is of the Capitol Building, and as I'm sure you're well aware of the many things that happened under the former president, DC became a very different city. More fences, more barriers and these old trucks used to block roadways in a very intimidating way. So, my encounter with the place, with public places and spaces became radically different. Well, many of the places ceased to be public spaces. There were concourses and avenues where you could walk around the Capitol. You could freely walk into many buildings, encounter people who were making the laws of the land. But for a long while, the police, the fences, the security, the ever-present helicopters overhead gave a very different feeling about these encounters going on in so-called public spaces. And it became more fraught with a great many dangers.

When we're thinking of encounters in space and time, in what form are these happening, these co-present encounters? And what shifts can we now talk about?

When we think about silence transforming into something else, cacophony into something else – to see how people express their anger and especially after George Floyd was murdered, to see what happened in public spaces at this time. Many people, as I'm sure you're aware, protested in public spaces, took over those spaces in response to the killing. Graffiti and street art were used very much as a form of communication and protest and encounter. I really wanted to think about how we've envisioned encounters and how our understanding is shifting, has evolved over time.

Gehan Selim

I'm an architect, I'm not an artist, but I can see how art plays a very important role in defining spaces as well and how artists sometimes struggle to visualise it. Similar practices have been happening in many other places so it's not really context specific, it's not really an issue a specific group or a specific community of artists have, but I can see this and I started to trace examples all over the world.

What came to mind was the Arab Spring in 2011 when artists were trying to draw graffiti on the walls in the public squares where the protests were happening, and suddenly after a couple of hours, all these were wiped out. And they don't exist anymore. And that kind of power and resistance from artists of keeping that emotional attachment to the space using art, they do to keep resonating their voices once again as a matter of power.

Partly what I do as well is understand how objects give us that impression of visualising space and visualising violence and struggle in public spaces. How do artists navigate the struggle? And what will be the additional challenges that would contribute to adding further silencing of this power into the space and adding more contradictions and tensions?

Who has the right to be in these spaces? How do we begin to challenge those limitations and create a space of belonging for everyone?

Khadijah Ibrahim

As an artist, when I'm looking at this aspect of space and liminal space, I'm thinking about bodies and buildings. I'm really thinking about access and accessibility to create. I'm also thinking about that room provided for us; and whenever we're in those spaces, we have to bring with us so much of the past, to bring into the future. So, this is an aspect of land, landscape, water and air, history and the atrocities upon the black body. And so the idea of my provocation really more than anything was the way in which we mark and remark and map out spaces that are accessible to various communities, accessible to humans. And then with that there are these limitations attached to it. So how do we see bodies in spaces? Who has the right to be in these spaces? How do we begin to challenge those limitations and create a space of belonging for everyone?

In answering your question, it's about redressing the past in order to move forward into the future, and thinking about whose responsibility it is. Is it the responsibility of the artist who creates work? As Nina Simone said, 'the artist's responsibility is to create art, to be the artist'. And yet with any art form, and anyone creating art, there is always a political side to it. There has to be. In my own work, I'm thinking about how these colonial traces of race and racism begin to separate and exclude.

I really like the idea of the Arab Spring and the way people were using graffiti to mark out aspects of their emotions, their feelings. The work that I was doing was looking at placards. If you stand in your own silence – because the silence of racism exists – it becomes very uncomfortable. So, sometimes we remove ourselves from not having those discussions. But what happens when you start to mark out the space? Is it a little bit like the Arab Spring when they were graffitiing their slogans? What happens if you stand in the space with a slogan, expressing an emotion? And what does that mean to the person reading it in the space, in the landscape? But also how these slogans can be easily erased, how graffiti can be erased, how language and expression can be erased. And so everything becomes politicised in that sense. And I guess what I'm examining is all the reasons behind why bodies are policed and politicised in the landscape, how we enter these buildings, who belongs in these buildings.

Nigel Rapport

'Becoming' is a key word. And part of my argument is that we have the capacity to 'become' as individuals. And we should have the right to become. Furthermore, no one can know ahead of time – and no one should have the power, or the right to claim ahead of time – what another individual's coming into their own, amid an individual lifetime, should entail. Which is why Iris Murdoch's beautiful notion that 'real compassion is agnosticism' is such a powerful one.[5] Also her notion of a good society as one that provides space in which individuals can become in their own way, space to discern what is good for them. According to Murdoch, what's fundamental to a good society is restraint and reticence.

Khadijah Ibrahim

How do we begin to combat racism? How do we begin to combat the concept of marginalised communities and enable them to come to the forefront and to be seen? The concept is also based around conversations which are often not had. The idea of my provocation is to be able to look at the way in which we address liminal spaces. How can a liminal space give speech to the people who are part of that space? How do we begin to give birth to listening to the artists? What is the role of the artist today?

I want to leave you with that thought of The Passover; the concept of passing over artists. The concept of liminal spaces, the concept of performance, the concept of dialogue. How do we move forward in the future? With that, I would want us to think about how we begin to not make promises but actually make changes for the future. I am an artist who has been practising for over 30 years and I still look at myself as a struggling artist trying to create work.

But also, how do we enter into a dialogue rather than just looking at a marginalised community, just looking at oppression? Because within the African and Caribbean community, we also like to discuss the idea and produce work around joy. Black joy. We like the idea of the collaboration of narratives from different communities. How do we begin to shape these ideas for the future? I'd like to open up the space to continue this dialogue of bodies in the landscape and unification for the future.

Mohasin Ahmed

When you include a wide 'other' group, you're met with issues because you're not specific enough. You will always attract the majority within the minority because the minority does not feel safe accessing that space. We can meet each other by catering to each other, listening to each other and recognising minorities within marginalised groups. Providing communities with the tools to create safe spaces and platforms for us, by us and on our terms allows us to feel safe enough to share our true selves with others. There's no feeling like being in a room full of strangers but feeling love, respect and safety, and this can only be replicated in spaces that serve that purpose.

When we think of clubbing, especially in the UK, negative connotations usually come to mind of drugs, drunkenness and disorderly behaviour. In my experience, these stereotypes are not entirely incorrect and that's why clubs didn't feel safe for me. And when you search Google images for DJs, typical images are of men, and while there's nothing inherently wrong with male DJs, when the space is created mostly by one demographic, it's usually tailored for that demographic. I want to think more about the space in which DJing happens and how music can facilitate empowerment for people to be authentically themselves.

DJing, like other musical pursuits, is a form of art and expression. At Mojxmma, I play music that predominates Queer culture for People of Colour (PoC). I play Queer Artists of Colour and use tempos and beats that are common across the African and Asian diaspora, as well as in voguing and the Queer ballroom scene. It's important for me to play this type of music, not just to spotlight those in the community but to facilitate creating a safe space. As these artists share their stories through their music, their stories are relatable and inspiring to us. We can dance with each other and with their lyrics and sound, we feel in a place of acceptance.

I also play music from other artists and genres that wouldn't normally be associated with Queer culture, for example UK grime and American hip hop, because although it's not usually made for us, we still enjoy it. However, the clubs that usually play this music are not safe for visibly Queer or femme-presenting people. We want to dance, we want to get drunk, we want to let go like everyone else; but we want to be safe from fear of discrimination and from the cishet male gaze. The atmosphere I aim to create at Mojxmma is like your best friend's house party. We play your favourite songs, you're surrounded by people like you and you feel safe and you feel accepted.

Sarah-Jane Mason

Lacuna Festivals (we/our) was founded in Lanzarote in 2019 as a festival run by and for practicing, contemporary artists. The ethos of the festival is that there is an intrinsic value in art that transcends differences and goes beyond its perceived monetary worth. The principle of equal opportunities for artists regardless of differentials is one of our core beliefs, and it is this founding principle that ensures encounters with the other are simply part and parcel of the festival experience. In the context of the festival, difference, or otherness, relates to differentials of any kind, whether delineated and defined by systemic or rational principles or arbitrary ideas. Difference is a tag that can be worn proudly, but it can also be a given label that becomes stuck, perhaps to someone who does not self-identify as different.

People Everywhere – Zita Holbourne / Paul Delpani – Lacuna Festivals Clash 2022

We do not want to add to this 'othering' of people or spaces and instead take steps to bring artists, audience members and venues together on a level playing field. Of course, we have to acknowledge that it is a challenge to negate prejudices and the allure of capital gain, in both ourselves and in festival participants. We scrutinise our decisions and ensure our actions are transparent to enable questioning and dialogue between ourselves as organisers and also with and between participants. These steps keep us accountable to the festival ethos and safeguard our belief that no one artist, audience member or venue is more or less important than any other.

Our goal is to hold space for everyone without an intrinsic, hierarchical structure to create levels of difference and otherness. Even when split into the arbitrary categories of artist, audience or venue, it is clear that all participants within each category are so very different; yet, we expect all festival participants to work within the same parameters: donations can be requested, but compulsory charges cannot be made; event numbers can be limited, but places must be accessible to all; artworks can be sold, but commissions cannot be taken. Building this culture of equality enables meaningful encounters with difference to occur with a lower possibility of them becoming threatening or hostile. Engaging with difference is something that all parties are doing and therefore it becomes the norm.

Kate Fellows

How do we in cultural organisations create a space where people can meet as individuals and when we can have multiple individuals meeting each other? How do we create a comfortability factor where we can recognise and celebrate the difference for shared learning? When we do it well, when we manage to hold that space, it's really awesome. One of our programmes is called Careers For All, and in that programme, we work with young people who are living with additional needs to provide them with meaningful work experience placements and opportunities. We work with the individual and their support workers to build a programme of life and work skills development to support and help them.

Now yes, as part of that they help us build exhibitions, help with school groups, with public engagement, with social media. But often for these individuals, the biggest learning comes from meeting other people in the workplace. Learning how to do things like interact in the staff room, be themselves in the office, travel to work on their own and get there on time. Take one individual whose main interest was in drawing animation artwork for comics. So, we structured a task that got them to do a little bit of other work balanced with being able to draw the collections because their structured learning was actually that the world of work often doesn't allow you to just do what you like – you have to do what your employer wants you to do. It's the softer side of work in effect. We create space for them to be themselves, be accepted, be nurtured; but also prepare them in a safe and supported space for that big bad world of work.

For us the learning is equally as powerful. The work has changed us as an organisation. It's altered our booking systems for mainstream schools, it's changed the questions we asked teachers, it's altered our approach to our wider programmes and made us more open to different routes of employment. Working alongside the individuals has really challenged some of my colleagues' views about young people and about individuals living with the label of autistic spectrum conditions, and it's made them reflect on their own views. For one colleague, it's given them the confidence to own their own experience and ask for extra support – something they've never disclosed before. All of these things make a better more welcoming museum service for everyone.

Ana Deumert

In our current moment, we now encounter each other digitally and not in person, not body to body. For me, online meetings are a huge challenge as a scholar. How can we understand them without naturalising them? During the course of yesterday, we spoke about the importance of bodies and embodiment – but what about our virtual embodiments? How do we understand our truncated torsos? What does it mean for an encounter to only see a person's face and upper body? Rosine spoke about a moment when she could only see her slides but could not see any of us. I've had similar moments in online presentations and found them deeply unsettling. In these moments, one feels almost as if one is alone in the world, and I would catch myself thinking, what would happen if I would just get up and leave?

In the context of my work on digital media, I've often wondered: do digital media, because of their technological affordances, create spaces for monologue rather than dialogue? For example, overlapping speech, something that is common and extremely meaningful in everyday interaction, is largely absent from our Zoom engagements. The discussion about digital encounters in the context of COVID also raises questions of who is excluded from such encounters and who is included and in what ways. So maybe in the current moment we would want to ask, what does the act of inclusion look like and sound like on Zoom, on WhatsApp, on Facebook and so forth?

But I still feel inspired by the ETHER (Ethics and Aesthetics of Encountering the Other) conference. It really provided hope and nourishment in a difficult time. The intellectual and emotional generosity of everyone was very special. Something so rare in academia. I do not use the word 'community' lightly – but I do feel that there was a community, maybe just fleetingly, but also very real despite the virtual/ digital complexities.

Notes

(1) Kubanyiova, M. and Creese, A. (2021) About ETHER – Ethics and aesthetics of encountering the other. See https://ether.leeds.ac.uk/about/ (accessed 29 April 2023).

(2) Alcoff, L.M. (2020) Lugones's world-making. *Critical Philosophy of Race* 8 (1–2), 199–211.

(3) Rapport, N. (2010) Apprehending anyone: The non-indexical, post-cultural and cosmopolitan human actor. *Journal of the Royal Anthropological Institute* 16 (1), 84–101.

(4) Rapport, N. (2012) *Anyone, The Cosmopolitan Subject of Anthropology.* Berghahn.

(5) Murdoch, I. (1962) *An Unofficial Rose.* Chatto and Windus.